BIG IDEAS
FOR
SMALL SPACES

BIG IDEAS
FOR
SMALL SPACES

CREATIVE IDEAS AND 30 PROJECTS FOR BALCONIES,
ROOF GARDENS, WINDOWSILLS AND TERRACES

KAY MAGUIRE & TONY WOODS
PHOTOGRAPHY BY JASON INGRAM

FIREFLY BOOKS

A FIREFLY BOOK

Published by Firefly Books Ltd. 2017

Design and layout copyright © 2017 Octopus Publishing Group Ltd.
Text copyright © 2017 The Royal Horticultural Society

First printing

Publisher Cataloging-in-Publication Data (U.S.)

A CIP record for this title is available from the Library of Congress

Library and Archives Canada Cataloguing in Publication

A CIP record for this title is available from Library and Archives Canada

Published in the United States by
Firefly Books (U.S.) Inc.
P.O. Box 1338, Ellicott Station
Buffalo, New York 14205

Published in Canada by
Firefly Books Ltd.
50 Staples Avenue, Unit 1
Richmond Hill, Ontario L4B 0A7

Printed and bound in China

First published by Mitchell Beazley,
a division of Octopus Publishing Group Ltd
Carmelite House, 50 Victoria Embankment
London EC4Y 0DZ

Published in association with the Royal
Horticultural Society
Publisher Alison Starling; **Editor** Pollyanna
Poulter; **Art Director** Juliette Norsworthy;
Designer Lizzie Ballantyne; **Photographer**
Jason Ingram; **Senior Production Controller**
Allison Gonsalves; **RHS Publisher** Rae
Spencer-Jones; **RHS Editor** Simon Maughan

KAY MAGUIRE

Kay Maguire is the author of the award-
winning, bestselling *RHS Grow Your
Own Crops in Pots*, which was published
in February 2013. She is a regular
contributor to gardening magazines
such as *BBC Gardeners' World*, *The
Garden* and *Amateur Gardening* as
well as being the video producer for
the RHS website. Kay trained at the
Royal Botanic Gardens, Kew, where
she gained the Kew Diploma, and was
the Horticultural Editor of the BBC's
Gardeners' World for six years. She is
now a freelance writer, editor, producer
and, most importantly, grower.

TONY WOODS

Garden designer Tony Woods, 31,
trained at Myerscough College and
set up his urban garden design
company, Garden Club London, at the
age of 26. The company specializes
in plant-focused garden design and
soft landscaping in an urban setting,
often on balconies, roof gardens, and
terraces. In 2013 he won the RHS's
Young Garden Designer of the Year
award for his impressive "Escape to
the City" garden at the Tatton Park
Flower Show. Monty Don of the BBC's
Gardeners' World described Tony as a
garden designer with "extraordinary
sureness of touch." In the summer of
2014 Tony designed a roof garden for
retailer John Lewis's 150th anniversary
celebrations at its flagship Oxford
Street store in London.

THE RHS

The Royal Horticultural Society (RHS)
is the UK's largest gardening charity,
dedicated to advancing horticulture
and promoting good gardening. Its
charitable work includes providing
expert advice and information, training
the next generation of gardeners and
promoting the ecological, aesthetic and
psychological benefits of gardening in
an urban environment.

CONTENTS

INTRODUCTION

There is no doubt that gardens are getting smaller.

Motivated by profit, developers of new housing estates give their properties increasingly tiny plots, and as more and more of us move to the cities and urban areas, houses are converted into apartments with little or no outside space and existing gardens are developed into further new housing, eating up the green space.

It can feel like the concrete and tarmac are starting to take over and this is not just a loss for us, in terms of gardens. It also has a huge impact on wildlife and the overall environment, not to mention our mental wellbeing and health.

But growing space is there if we look for it. It's on the walls and roofs around us, on windowsills and down narrow passageways. And although all of these sites have challenges, they are by no means impossible to overcome. All over the world people are grabbing outside space on fire escapes, ledges and walls and creating beautiful productive gardens.

Our aim in this book is to show you all the places where it is possible to grow plants, and to offer practical solutions to greening these otherwise barren, sterile spots. We have come up with 30 inspiring but simple projects to help you make creative use of every bit of the space you've got — no matter whether it's a wall, a tiny patio, a balcony or a roof. Some of the projects are more ambitious than others but all are intended for the first-time grower, as well as the more experienced gardener who has downsized to a much smaller plot.

If you don't have a traditional garden or yard, it can be easy to think that gardening is not for you, but everyone and anyone can grow something, no matter how cramped their space, and this book will show you how.

Left: Tony Woods (left) and Kay Maquire (right) love the challenge of turning even the trickiest space into a place where plants will thrive.

Opposite: Even the smallest space can become a beautiful floral garden.

GARDEN ANYWHERE

SECTION 1

WHY SMALL SPACES ARE DIFFERENT

Below: **In a small space** it is often best to keep to a clear design and a simple color palette. Trees and climbers draw the eye up and away from boundaries and neighboring plots, while lush, bold plants give an intimate jungle feel.

When you're making inventive and creative use of the space around you, you are often forced to garden and grow in places that are not ideal. In a large garden you have the freedom to choose where your plants go and how to divide up the space according to your requirements. Plants are grown in the open, away from rain shadows and shade as much as possible; garbage cans and compost bins are hidden from view; and boundaries hold little influence over your design.

But the smaller the space, the less flexible it becomes and the greater the challenge for the grower. On a tiny patio, roof terrace, or in a stairwell you are stuck with what you've got. The site may be overlooked by passers-by or be next to a busy road; it might be shrouded in shade, battered by the wind, or scorched by the sun. Perhaps it's just a windowsill or an awkward passageway running next to the house. All of these are typical challenges faced by the small-space grower, yet they definitely do not make an area impossible to cultivate.

Start to see every outdoor surface and spare ground as potential growing space and you're halfway there.

Above: **The raised beds** around the edge of this rooftop garden are filled with wispy grasses and the elegant spikes of *Gaura lindheimeri*, which provide privacy without blocking the view completely.

Designers have come up with all sorts of clever and imaginative tricks to make a space look bigger, brighter, or longer, and you can always rely on plants for their incredible adaptability. A whole range of trees, shrubs, and perennials have evolved in the most remarkable ways to tolerate harsh conditions, and you will find that whatever challenge your particular site holds, there are plenty of exciting plants that will grow there.

MICROCLIMATES

Every garden has its own individual microclimate, which is often quite different from that of the surrounding area. Even within a garden there will be distinct areas, each with its own conditions, and when you're growing in unusual and innovative spaces, such microclimates can be even more pronounced.

Many things can influence the microclimates within a plot. It's crucial to know exactly what range of conditions you have so that you choose the right design and the best plants to grow there.

The **aspect** of your space — whether it faces south or north, and the way the sunlight moves across it — will create different pockets of sun and shade, warmth and cool. In the northern hemisphere, a south-facing wall will be warm and dry, baked by the sun for most of the day, while a north-facing one, shrouded in shade, will be quite the opposite. East-facing walls are bathed in the morning sun, and walls that face west warm up slowly, catching the sun only at the end of the day.

Any space that is elevated or exposed such as a windowsill, balcony, and rooftop is likely to be battered by high **winds**. Such blustery conditions can also be a problem in side yards and passages, where the wind gets funnelled through tall buildings and whipped along these drafty corridors. Wind not only damages and desiccates plants but also lowers temperatures. It can turn an otherwise peaceful haven into a cold, uncomfortable one.

Conversely, gardens crammed in and surrounded by buildings are often protected from the wind, and this **shelter** can increase temperatures, making a space warmer than its surroundings so that a broader range of slightly tender plants will grow there.

The individual **features** within a garden will create mini-microclimates too. Buildings, trees, and tall plantings provide a natural windbreak, creating shelter and making it less cold, yet they can also cast **shade**. This can lead to cooler, damp conditions, while spots in a rain shadow in the lee of a wall or balcony will be parched and dry.

WIND

Wind is one of a gardener's biggest enemies. Although often associated with plots by the coast it can be a problem with small spaces too.

Any growing area high up is exposed to the wind, so growers on balconies, rooftops, and windowsills will all have to brace themselves against it. But down on the ground, narrow plots, hemmed in by buildings such as patios, side yards, and passageways, can suffer too. Wind trapped by buildings is forced through these narrow channels, building up speed and damaging any plants that are in its way. It shreds foliage, breaks fragile stems, and scorches leaves. It stunts and slows the growth of trees and shrubs and halts young plant development completely. Wind dries out plants and potting mix, lowers temperatures, and prevents pollinating insects from reaching plants.

But wind doesn't have to deter you from gardening. There are many plants that have adapted to being whipped by the wind, but erecting a simple shelter against it first can have a miraculous effect. Always use a semi-permeable shelter (that is, one that is only 50 percent solid), which will filter the wind, rather than a solid fence or wall, which will block the wind and cause further problems. When wind hits a solid force it bounces up and then over it, landing heavily on the other side with even greater force and turbulence

Hedging with wind-tolerant plants, and screens made from woven bamboo or rush, as well as willow and hazel hurdles, are all perfect shelterbelt material and will make a huge difference in the range of plants you can grow. (See p145 for plants that can tolerate wind.)

Plants, particularly trees, in pots have a habit of toppling over in strong winds, especially when the trees are in leaf, as the leaves act like sails. Anchor any pots down.

SHADE

When you're eking out growing space, it may often be overshadowed by something. Walls, trees, and buildings all cast shade, which can also be found at the base of a hedge, in a dank corner of a patio, or beneath a neighbor's balcony. A plot facing north or east could be shrouded in shade for most, if not all, of the day.

Plants need sunlight to survive but the amount they require varies. Many have adapted to cope with different light levels, while lots of plants grow perfectly well in shade even though they prefer full sun (they'll just produce fewer flowers or fruit). All plants have their own light level preferences, but whichever depth of shade you have there will be something gorgeous to grow in it. If

Left: **Growing in a place** that is exposed to the wind can be one of the most challenging sites for a gardener. Fortunately plants such as these New Zealand flax (*Phormium tenax*) have adapted to cope with it.

An area is described as in **full sun** when it is open to the sun for most of the day and is not shaded by trees and buildings.

Partial shade is a spot that is open to the sky but direct sunlight is blocked by trees or walls. It may still receive 2–6 hours of full sun each day as the sun moves across the sky.

Light shade is a site that receives sun for only a couple of hours a day, while **dappled shade** is the blotchy shade cast by the foliage of trees.

Dense shade is the darkest area, where tall buildings and trees block the light for most or all of the day. Dense shade is often found beneath evergreen trees — the classic dry shade at the base of a leylandii tree or at the base of a wall.

Above: **The bright globes** of white alliums popping up through a carpet of lady's mantle add a flash of light to this shady spot.

you improve your soil with a generous helping of well-rotted compost, your plant options will increase.

The key is to know the depth and type of shade that is cast across your plot. Once you have worked this out you'll learn which plants you can grow. Watch your plot and note the main areas of sun and shade throughout the day. Shade from an evergreen tree or a high wall can be parched and dense, while the dappled shade beneath a deciduous tree can be moist enough to take the edge off a bright summer's day.

Far left: **Plants with white flowers** such as this hydrangea are a wise choice in a shady garden. When surrounded by a tapestry of green leaves they stand out and catch the eye.

Left: **Ferns are well known** for their love of shade, and there are hundreds to select from, in a variety of sizes and leaf colors, that will add gorgeous textures and hues to a gloomy spot.

Above left: **A dense hedge** is an effective barrier against both the noise and air pollution that can occur when your garden is close to a busy road.

Above right: **When access is tight** use a number of smaller planters rather than just one or two large ones — they will have just as much impact, without the effort and strain of moving heavy pots.

POLLUTION

Growing spaces that are open to the elements — a front garden, rooftop, balcony, or windowsill — can all suffer from exposure to pollution, and for the plants that are growing under flight paths, next to busy roads, and near factories the accompanying dirt, grime, and fumes can be a significant problem.

As traffic thunders past a windowsill or is held up in a traffic jam beside a patio area, deposits from vehicle exhausts settle on plant leaves. Salt from the road splashes onto them, while chemical deposits, dust, and particulates in the air cover them in dirt, clog leaves, and block pores, thereby reducing photosynthesis and each plant's ability to take up water.

For many plants this will stunt and weaken growth, making them more vulnerable to attack from pests and diseases. It will also reduce flowering and fruiting and eventually lead to premature death.

If pollution is an issue, protect your plants by erecting a shelterbelt around them (see p12 and p145). Otherwise, opt for plants that are tolerant of airborne pollution: berberis, holly, and cotoneaster are all tough plants that will thrive in a hedge and help to shelter your plot.

ACCESS

How you get into a very small space, and therefore how you bring in plants, trees, pots, tools, and anything else you might need, can be a real struggle. Many can be reached only by going through the house or by navigating narrow doorways or steep stairways. This can make carrying bulky, heavy loads difficult, if not impossible. Therefore always check access points before you plan anything, and measure the width of doorways, windows, passages, and stairways.

Unless you can find some way to overcome access problems, the route into your space will dictate exactly what you can and can't have in it, and as a result the whole feel of the space itself. It will influence the size and type of materials you use and the plants you grow.

If you're not doing major building work and just want to bring in plants, potting mix, and pots, check if there are any other ways of getting everything in. Ask friendly neighbors if you can lift things over their walls or through their windows. It may be possible to winch things up the outside of the building rather than lugging it up endless narrow stairways. But, whichever way you go, always protect your access points — put down plastic sheeting and protect doorframes with cardboard and tape.

WATER

Access to water can be a big problem when you're growing plants in a place that isn't typically a garden or where they would usually grow. Growing spaces created on rooftops, stairwells, windowsills, and passageways are unlikely to be anywhere near a water source, let alone an outdoor tap. They are also often exposed to high winds, baking sun, and rain shadows, all of which can leave plants parched and desperate for a drink.

Lack of water is the main cause of death in plants, and in small spaces many things can cause drought. Ideally plants are grown in sheltered spots away from the shade and shadow cast by buildings, trees, and walls, but in small spaces this is rarely possible. High winds on balconies, rooftops, and windowsills dry out compost as well as desiccate and damage leaves, thereby reducing their ability to take up water. Down on the ground, surrounding structures and nearby trees cast rain shadows, which prevent water from reaching your plants. In these situations watering can become a demanding, almost full-time job, and if you don't have a tap nearby, you can be driven to despair. Fortunately there are ways to make watering less of an issue.

- Wherever possible install an outdoor tap (faucet) — lugging endless watering cans back and forth through the house is enough to make anyone despair. If this is impossible, collect water where you can — off gutters and by diverting downpipes into water tanks, whether store-bought or home-made. Recycling gray water from sinks and baths can also help, as long as you use eco-friendly detergents and soaps. (For more water-saving tips see p155.)
- Before you even consider a windowbox ensure it can be watered easily — either from inside your home or with a long-handled hose from outside.
- Always grow the right plant for your space. Choose plants that can cope with drying winds, high levels of heat, and drought.
- Make sure you grow plants in the best soil or potting mix — one that is moisture-retentive but free-draining is ideal. Dig in well-rotted garden compost or other organic matter if you need to improve its structure.
- Mulch everything. A layer of garden compost, chipped bark, even grass clippings will lock moisture in the soil and prevent it from evaporating and drying out.
- Weed regularly to stop weeds from competing with your plants for moisture.

Right: **Having a water source** close by is essential wherever you are growing. If it is not possible to install an outdoor tap, a water barrel is a great substitute.

TRICKS TO MINIMIZE WEIGHT

- Use fiberglass and plastic pots rather than terracotta, metal, and stone.
- Line containers with styrofoam chips and old plastic pots as drainage material, instead of adding weighty gravel or terracotta pieces.
- Choose multipurpose potting mix rather than a heavier, soil-based one.
- Attach pots to adjacent walls rather than sitting them on the ground so that the walls support the weight and not the roof or balcony.
- Keep pots at the edges of your space where they will have a higher load-bearing capacity, rather than dotting them around the middle.

WEIGHT

Any surface that's not on the ground and was not intended to support plants or a garden can involve weight issues. Balconies, rooftops, even windowsills are all reliant on the strength of the buildings that support them. Therefore, before you do anything, check how much weight your space can take.

The title deeds of your home may give you information on the load-bearing capacity of your roof or balcony; otherwise a structural engineer or architect can advise on the strength of your space, the load it can take, and the best way to distribute that weight.

All plants, even a lawn, need soil to sustain them — on average shrubs require a depth of 30–45cm (12–18in) of soil to thrive, while trees can demand a depth of up to 1m (3ft). However soil is heavy, and even more so when it's wet. Add this together with the weight of the containers, drainage material, and mulch — plus any accessories such as seating, tables, and barbecues — and they will all start to take their toll.

PRIVACY

Neighboring buildings, windows, balconies, or people passing by often look out onto small gardens and the lack of privacy can become a real source of irritation. When a growing space is created among buildings and

Below: **Despite being out in the open**, this narrow fire escape has become a thriving green oasis providing a degree of privacy.

on rooftops it can feel particularly exposed, and it can be a considerable challenge to overcome this without making your space feel enclosed, dark, and out of context with its environment.

Wherever you are growing, make a note of any area that is most open to the public gaze and concentrate your focus there. The trick is to create a feeling of privacy, yet still let in the light and retain the views.

Use semi-transparent screening such as woven willow and hazel or else plan a living fence with plants and hedging rather than erecting a solid barrier, which blocks everything out. Grow climbers on trellis or up obelisks to create a sense of height around you. Plant containers with light, airy plants such as grasses and palms, and mix these with denser plantings of boxwood (*Buxus*) and other evergreen shrubs.

If the privacy problem comes from a patio being viewed from above, or a balcony from below, grow trees if you have the room or build a pergola or arbor to mask your growing area.

Remember that plants change with the seasons. For example, deciduous trees and shrubs lose their leaves each year but at a time when you may not be outside so often and so may be less bothered by being seen. Meanwhile evergreen trees and other plants that provide year-round screening will also cast dense shade. A balanced combination of both types is a good solution.

Right: **Semi-transparent plants such as** this palm (*Trachycarpus fortunei*) help to provide some privacy without making the space feel hemmed in.

WHY GET GROWING?

Plants transform our lives in so many ways. They add vibrancy and color, clean the air we breathe, insulate buildings, and bring wildlife closer. They can help us make friends, keep our houses safe, and, remarkably, cut down on crime. Bringing plants into our lives through gardening enables us to benefit from all of these things — and you don't need acres of land to be able to do so.

You may be lucky enough to have a small balcony, a patio garden, or a roof you could use for planting. You may have only a windowsill, but the simple pleasure of growing a few tomatoes or a basket full of flowers is the same wherever they're positioned, and the motivation for doing so is also the same.

People start gardening for lots of reasons such as a wish to grow their own food or get fit. They know that gardening connects them with nature and makes them happy and healthy, and they just want to give it a try.

If you're not already convinced of the benefits, we aim with this chapter to highlight the many things that make gardening so great and why.

No matter where you live and what outdoor space you have, you can give it a try.

BEAUTY

One of the main incentives to start growing is the simple desire, if not need, to have plants around us, because plants are beautiful. All year round, they present us with something wonderful to look at. From the first green shoots of spring bulbs pushing through the earth, the ruby-red of strawberries waiting to be picked in summer, and fluffy golden seedheads to the fiery tints of leaves in autumn and the sprinkling of frost on a bare stem in winter, nature paints a glorious picture for us every single day.

Plants bring color — in endless shades of green and joyous hues; texture — from spikes to fluffy seedheads; noise — whispering, rustling grasses and rattling seed pods. Plants add vitality and spirit to our lives, and as human beings, and once upon a time hunter-gatherers (albeit 10,000 years ago), we are innately and instinctively drawn to them. Nature is something we need and if we can have it near us, by growing and gardening ourselves, so much the better.

Opposite: **Even a simple windowbox** can bring nature into our lives and brighten our days. This spring box planted with bulbs and evergreens will lift the spirits.

Left: **Plants add jubilant color** and zing. The achillea, dahlia, and persicaria in this raised planter will burst into bloom in midsummer and carry on their display until they are knocked back by the first frosts.

Above: **Growing your own food** is a great way to start gardening, and easy, speedy vegetables such as radishes will give you a fresh home-grown crop in just a few weeks.

Below far left: **Seedheads touched** by a sprinkling of frost are a stunning sight on a winter's morning.

Below left: **Gardening is a great way** to get closer to nature and wildlife. Just one pot of lavender will bring the bees buzzing to your space.

Left: **The plants on this** greened roof not only look good but also help to reduce the urban temperatures and keep the building below warmer in winter and cooler in the summer.

THE ENVIRONMENT

Plants and gardens play a vital part in our lives but they have a beneficial effect on the environment too, particularly in our towns and cities. The presence of green space, however small, is proven to reduce temperatures, insulate buildings, and prevent urban flooding, and the more of them there are, the better.

Towns and cities are naturally warmer in spring and summer than the cooler suburbs and countryside. This "heat island" effect is due to the combination of heat-absorbing surfaces (such as roads, roofs, pavements, and walls) and the heat coming from cars and buildings.

Conveniently, trees and other plants can help to regulate these high temperatures. The shade they cast cools the air, as does the water that is naturally lost through their leaves (in a process called evapotranspiration). Streets and neighborhoods with gardens and green spaces are considerably cooler in summer than streets without them. These lower temperatures not only reduce the dangers that high temperatures can pose to human heath but also cut down on the need for air conditioning and therefore energy consumption.

Plants can help keep us warm in winter too. Trees and hedges act as windbreaks, creating shelter and protection against cold winds, while green walls and roofs are particularly useful in insulating buildings, thereby keeping down heat costs and reducing energy use.

Trees and other plants, and the soil they grow in, also assist in preventing urban flooding. Without plants and soil to soak it up, rainwater simply runs off roofs and hard surfaces and flows into the drains nearby. In times of heavy rain this can increase pressure on the drains and eventually lead to flooding. Plants on the ground in beds and borders and on green roofs and walls catch this rain and help to slow down run-off and the demands that it puts on urban drainage.

HEALTH

Gardening is good for you! Horticultural therapists have long understood the positive health benefits that gardening brings. Just looking at plants and gardens makes us feel better, while the act of gardening is good for the soul — it has been proven to lower blood pressure, increase brain activity, and leave us with a heightened sense of wellbeing.

Gardening assists us in staying connected with the seasons and the natural world. This is critical for our mental wellbeing but it is also a brilliant distraction, taking our minds off whatever is bothering us as we pluck out weeds, water pots, and tie in plants. There is a natural motivation to get out and do something when you have plants to tend — often year-round — and you get a wonderful sense of satisfaction and achievement as you work.

But gardening isn't just relaxing; it is great for physical health too. The energetic activity of gardening increases the heart rate, stretches muscles, and gives us a good workout every time we pick up a spade, keeping us fit and our joints strong. And if you grow your own food, you are more likely to eat better — and appreciate fresh, healthy, vitamin-packed fruit and vegetables that are free from chemicals and air miles.

Below left: **Tending to a garden**, with all the digging, weeding, and watering this entails, is a satisfying and rewarding way to keep fit.

Below right: **Growing your own food** is a great way to ensure you enjoy plenty of fresh fruit and vegetables.

Bottom right: **A garden can stimulate** all the senses, and listening to the soothing sound of a trickling fountain is a particularly lovely way to relax.

Top left: **Trees act as signposts** for birds, indicating that there is somewhere to rest and roost, as well as food to eat.

Top right: **Providing habitats** for insects such as this bug hotel will help to attract overwintering ladybugs, lacewings, and solitary bees to your space.

Above left and Below right: **Even a tiny garden pond** can become home to aquatic life such as newts and frogs.

Above center: **Grow a broad range** of nectar-rich flowering plants to ensure pollinating insects such as butterflies and bees are regular visitors to your garden.

Right center: **Make a home** for solitary bees by bunching hollow canes and hanging them in a sheltered sunny spot.

WILDLIFE

As natural habitats disappear or shrink in the countryside, gardens and other green spaces have become increasingly important as a refuge and alternative habitat for our wildlife. The diversity of plants they contain makes them invaluable for a whole range of insects, birds, and other creatures. Even the smallest windowbox, crammed full of flowers, will support pollinators such as bees, butterflies, and lacewings.

You don't need a dedicated wildlife garden, or even a garden, to encourage wildlife. All creatures need food, shelter, and somewhere to breed, and simply by growing plants you provide a habitat in which they can do this. If there are enough of these habitats, however small, they link together into green corridors and give wildlife the room to roam and search for food, mates, and shelter.

Helping wildlife assists humans too. Many visiting insects such as hoverflies, butterflies, bees, and

SUPPORTING WILDLIFE

- Grow flowers, both native and non-native, but particularly those with single and nectar-rich blooms, which will attract butterflies, bees, and lacewings.
- Plant a tree — even just one — and you provide a wealth of food for countless insects, small mammals, and birds. A tree's height makes it easily spotted by birds, and it signals that green space and shelter, nesting sites, and possibly a snack or two are down below.
- Hedges, thickets, and walls and fences smothered in climbers are favorite places for roosting, sheltering, and breeding; if you pick the right plants, they can provide a tasty treat too.
- Leave seedheads and all those brown, fading stems where they are at the end of the season. They become essential food and homes for wildlife over the winter.
- Get composting — not just for you and your soil but for the endless worms, invertebrates, hedgehogs, and other creatures that will love it as a source of food and shelter.
- Create a pond. Even a small pond in a pot will provide water to drink and a habitat for amphibians and insects. It will also bring wonderful, buzzing life to your space.
- Leave out food for wildlife: for example, seeds and nuts for the birds; and meaty dog food for hedgehogs.
- Put out homes such as nesting boxes for birds, and "hotels" for bees.

lacewings are pollinators that enable our flowers to set seed, to fruit, and to grow again next year, while others such as ladybugs and hedgehogs are natural predators that provide vital assistance in our battle against problem pests.

POLLUTION

Car fumes, aircraft flying overhead, and the rumble of traffic are all synonymous with the stress of urban living, yet incredibly plants can be instrumental in helping us deal with and reduce these problems. Many shrubs and trees are tolerant of quite extreme urban pollution, and shrewd use and placement of them can have an almost magical effect.

All plants absorb carbon dioxide and convert it into oxygen, and they also filter the air very effectively. Leaves, stems, and branches trap particles in the air and absorb gaseous pollutants, which are then washed down to the ground by the rain. This enables us to breathe in less toxic air.

Plants are great sound guzzlers too and can be used to block out and muffle any nearby noise. A layer of climbers or pockets full of plants on a wall, a dense hedge — even a row of evergreens in pots — will act as a buffer to irritating, local noise and help to dampen down the sound.

Below: **Many plants,** such as this bottlebrush (*Callistemon*) are very effective at screening and absorbing pollution.

CRIME

Gardens and other green spaces enhance an area. A green neighborhood is a welcoming and attractive environment, and there is more likely to be a greater sense of joy, community, and pride felt by the people who have created those green spaces and all those who live there. People have more respect for green streets than those where there are no plants, trees, and gardens, and there is evidence that crime, graffiti, and litter are less likely to be found in green neighborhoods.

Amazingly plants themselves can also be used to stop crime. A canny choice of an impenetrable, prickly hedge on a boundary, spiky plants beneath windows, or a climbing rose up a drainpipe will make burglars think twice before choosing your home as an easy target.

Below: **Thorny *Pyracantha* spp.** planted beneath a window or on a boundary is a great deterrent against intruders.

Above right: **This narrow strip** of garden, crammed with plants, makes this street a more welcoming and pleasant place to be.

Opposite left: **A windowbox** full of jolly dahlias instantly brightens the gray.

Opposite right: **Hanging baskets** and windowboxes can have a hugely positive impact on a street and how it is viewed by visitors and residents alike.

COMMUNITY

It's a simple fact — plants and nature make us feel good, and their presence in our street or neighborhood means that it feels like a better, more vibrant place to live. Trees changing color with the season, hanging baskets cascading with joyous blooms, or pots plump with tomatoes are all it takes to raise a smile and instill a sense of wellbeing.

Property prices have always been higher in areas near parks or on tree-lined streets, and anywhere with outdoor space commands a premium. You may not have a typical yard but grab one where you can and feel the difference — not just to your own inner joy but also for your neighbors and passers-by who will experience it too.

Tending to the marigolds on your windowsill or tying in beans in the front garden is also a great way to meet the neighbors. Before you know it you may well be swapping gardening advice — even seeds or plants.

As well as bringing people together, gardens are also "catching." It's very common for a windowbox, planted balcony, or well-tended front garden to spark the gardening bug in others, and suddenly a whole street or stairwell has become a jubilant jungle of green. And so it goes on — that jungle improves the quality of life for everyone around it, injects a sense of community pride in the area, and before you know it you have a safe, desirable place in which to live.

TOP TIPS FOR COMMUNITY PLANTING

Your windowbox, hanging basket or front garden can be all it takes to inspire others in your street to start growing plants too. Join forces with a couple of neighbors and you could mobilize the whole street to get involved.

If you do decide to create a community group, however small, you are not alone. Neighborhoods of people all over the country are coming together to grow plants and green up their streets.

If you want to give it a try
- Distribute pamphlets to neighbors to keep them informed and encourage them to join in.
- Get help from your local council, gardening and wildlife groups, and nearby parks and gardens. They should be able to give you help and advice, may well offer donations of plants, seeds, potting mix, even money, and at the very least will know other organizations that can help you.
- Keep things simple. Hanging baskets, windowboxes and planting around the base of street trees are an easy but eye-catching way to get started.
- Grow low-maintenance plants. Opt for perennials and evergreens rather than demanding annual bedding plants that need constant watering, feeding, and deadheading to keep them looking good
- Drought-tolerant plants (see p147) will save you hours in watering, particularly in summer
- Naturalize bulbs in grass strips and under trees — they don't cost much, are easy to grow, and look amazing year after year.
- Scatter wildflower seed around to create meadows in bare areas of ground.
- Always ensure you have the landowner's permission before you start growing plants anywhere else other than in your own space.

Below: **Wildflowers from seeds** scattered at the base of street trees will transform an otherwise drab urban area.

MAKING THE MOST OF YOUR SPACE

You can garden anywhere. Wherever your outdoor space and whatever its size, it is possible to grow something there. Plants can thrive on the smallest windowsill or the most jaw-dropping roof space, but in small spaces it is all about making the most of what you've got.

Every bit of ground is invaluable but so are other flat surfaces. Start to view every surface — both horizontal and vertical — as potential growing space. Inventive gardeners have been transforming rooftops into beautiful gardens for years, but the creative planting of shed roofs, even the roofs of bird houses, with mats of sedum (see pp116–7) is an increasingly common sight, while the fashion for vertical planting and green walls is currently at its peak.

The slightest, narrowest passage or stairway — no matter how dank or neglected — can be transformed, while a lack of soil doesn't need to limit your ability to garden.

Containers have revolutionized the gardening potential of small spaces and are one of the easiest ways to get started. They can be the sole growing space or else form part of a larger planting scheme, and be as simple or ambitious as you wish.

Below: **Even the narrowest,** trickiest spot can become a thriving haven of green. No matter what size or shape of plot you have it is possible to grow plants there.

Above left: **Pots of seasonal flowering** plants, such as pansies and daffodils, can be brought into view when in flower and then replaced once they fade.

Above center: **Large containers**, such as this recycled lead trough, make attractive raised beds.

Above right: **Edible plants** make for beautiful thriving container features.

CONTAINER GROWING

When space and, most crucially, soil are limited, gardeners have to rely on creativity and imagination to grow plants wherever they can. On balconies, rooftops, and patios, there is rarely any earth to grow plants in. Therefore containers are the best way to bring life to these otherwise barren spaces.

If you have the room, raised beds (see p30) are a great way to create larger growing sites, but when your growing space is restricted to a tiny balcony or windowsill you'll find that pots and containers are the answer.

In many situations containers simply are all the garden you have and the only option when there is no soil at all. They're also invaluable when soil is poor or unsuitable for the plants you want to grow. You may yearn to try acid-loving blueberries or camellias but have alkaline soil, or else you may love carrots but have

stony ground. In these situations, you can grow them in containers and give your plants whatever soil they need to thrive.

Pots are also great for containing spreading or self-seeding plants such as mint or forget-me-nots. This is an important advantage in a small space where you really don't want one plant to take over.

Containers are amazingly versatile, allowing you to shift plants around, bringing them to the fore when they're in season and swapping them around as they fade. If you need a quick boost, plant a pot and it will lift your mood and bring a flash of color almost instantly.

An additional advantage of pots and other containers is that they are for small-scale growing and therefore comparatively low maintenance and easy to look after. This makes them ideal for novice and time-pressed gardeners.

CONTAINER CONSIDERATIONS

- Remember that plants in containers are living off a limited supply of food and water and they rely on us to keep those supplies topped up. Container growing is not for the forgetful!
- Always choose a big enough pot — the more soil there is, the more nutrients plants will receive, and the more room there will be for their roots to spread and grow. A larger volume of potting mix will also dry out less and help to insulate plant roots in cold weather.

Above left: **Bold, architectural** raised beds such as this example are a modern way to display plants when growing space in the ground is limited.

Above right: **The nasturtium** spilling over the edge of this weathered wooden bed emphasizes its height and makes the most of every bit of growing space.

RAISED BEDS

In spaces that have little, poor, or no soil a raised bed is the next best thing to growing in the ground. Although a familiar sight on vegetable plots and community gardens, raised beds can in fact be used anywhere, in any shape or size, and all plants — from edibles to ornamentals — will grow in them. They can be purchased in a range of self-assembly, pre-made kits in wood, metal, and plastic, but you can easily make your own out of scaffolding boards, railroad ties, pallets, or gabions (see pp124–6).

Ideally their width should be less than 1.5m (5ft) across because it's handy if you can reach across your bed to harvest, water, and weed rather than having to walk on it and compact the soil.

Raised beds can be any height, from one timber width upwards, but 40–50cm (16–20in) is a good size if you want to perch on the edges while you are working. Bearing this in mind, an edge with a width of 10cm (4in) is enough if you want just a quick rest, but if you wish your raised bed to double up as a seat (see pp114–5) — a brilliantly creative use of valuable space — then 20cm (8in) is a more comfortable width.

Raised beds do not need to stand on soil, it is not essential. They can be laid on concrete and hard standing, but before adding the soil always make sure you include a layer of drainage material, such as gravel on the base, to prevent the bed from becoming waterlogged. Also, drill drainage holes, using a flat drill bit 1–2cm (½–¾in) wide, making holes 5cm (2in) above ground level and 30cm (12in) apart all around the sides.

ADVANTAGES OF RAISED BEDS

- As with container growing, you can give plants the very best growing medium in a raised bed, rather than relying on what you have in the garden. You can also tailor it to suit whatever you wish to grow.
- Raised beds are easier to look after than pots simply by being bigger and containing more soil.
- They naturally have good drainage so the soil within them warms up quicker than soil in the ground. This means you can start planting a little earlier than you would in the open ground. Because of their good drainage they can also dry out quicker so do pay attention to watering.
- Plants in raised beds are more confined than they are in the open ground and therefore easier to manage — making them perfect for plants that are invasive or have a tendency to sprawl and spread. It is also easier to protect plants with netting so you can give them the extra help they might need in the battle against pests and diseases.
- Because plants are raised up they are brought closer to hand and view, making harvesting simpler and allowing you to get a closer look at your favorites. Raised beds are also helpful for those who have restricted mobility because there is no need for any bending to reach the plants.
- Plants are less likely to be targeted by pests, such as slugs and snails.
- You can grow plants more closely together than you would be able to in the ground.

WALLS

Almost everywhere has some vertical space around it. By extending your planting area to buildings and boundary walls, you will increase your growing space considerably — without taking up the ground space below.

Vertical growing makes a real feature of buildings and boundaries, raising plants up, so it is easier to appreciate a flower, to smell its scent, or to harvest fruit and vegetables, but it has practical advantages too. Plants growing on walls benefit from better air circulation than they would when growing on the ground, and they suffer less from pests and diseases. Also, the added layer of plants will insulate your walls, reduce air temperatures, and provide shade.

If you think of your space as an outdoor room, using walls for growing makes perfect sense, and the opportunities and ways to do this suddenly become endless.

Below: **The growing potential of walls** is too often missed but they can be easily transformed — in this case by a repeat display of pansies on creative shelving.

Climbing plants are the most obvious way to green a wall, and horizontal wires and trellis are easy to attach above beds, planters, and containers. Once plants are established this is one of the simplest and cheapest ways to bring color and interest to bare walls.

Gardening on the walls themselves has become a recent trend, and designers and amateur gardeners alike have been coming up with a whole host of ingenious ways of growing both up and down.

Pots of any style, planted with trailing plants and simply hung onto brackets or hooks can look stunning (see pp82–3), and when lined out on shelving or staging they will clothe a wall beautifully (see pp84–6). For denser cover, store-bought pocket planters ready for filling (see pp64–5) are available to buy in a variety of materials, colors, and styles. You can also customize containers and salvaged materials so that you have a look that's all your own.

String gutters across walls at different heights (see pp62–3), hang up wooden pallets (see pp56–7), and pack them with plants, or experiment with bricks, pipes, or cinder blocks. Whichever you choose, vertical growing will add shape, texture, and character to your plot.

Bear in mind the orientation of your wall when choosing which plants to grow, because it may be completely different from the rest of your garden. Walls are typically in shade for at least some of the day (although the top of a wall will often get more light than its base) and are frequently in rain shadows, so take care to assess the unique microclimate of your wall.

WINDOWSILLS

Windowsills may be all you have for growing, or they may be areas of much needed extra space. Although traditionally filled with bedding plants, such as petunias and pansies, there's no reason why windowsills can't be planted with bright perennials, scented herbs, and quick-growing edibles to become miniature gardens in their own right.

Measure your sill first and then find the biggest, deepest windowbox you can. Store-bought ones in plastic, stone, and wood are available, or customize your own boxes, crates, pots, and baskets to suit your space and style (see pp102–5).

Below left: **A simple wall pot** planted with tiarella and Japanese painted fern (*Athyrium niponicum* var. *pictum*) brings year-round color and life.

Below right: **You will always** have something to enjoy when you mix seasonal plants, such as petunias and verbena, with evergreens.

Left: **Trailing plants** at the front of a windowbox help to soften the edges of the container as well as green the wall below.

Although windowsill growing involves similar planting and maintenance to any form of container gardening, it does have its own set of challenges too.

Access: You need to be able to tend to and water your plants easily, preferably by leaning out of your window. However, if your windowbox is tricky to reach, you could water from the ground with a long-handled hose attachment, install drip irrigation, or look for pots with a built-in reservoir.

Drainage: Whichever container you use, make sure it has sufficient drainage holes in the base, and use free-draining potting mix.

Weight: Heavy pots offer more stability but check the strength of your windowsill before positioning.

Levels: Ensure your box is level, and prevent it from slipping down on a sloping sill by adding wedges or blocks to the base at the front.

Security: Always secure your box with metal brackets or hooks and wires

stretched across the front to stop it from falling off in high winds (and seriously hurting or damaging anyone or anything below). These will also deter people from stealing it.

Plant choice: Conditions can be tough up high, and exposure to wind, drought, and extremes of temperature will influence your choice of plants. On a windowsill the view from inside often matters more than the view from below, and the choice of plants and where they go within the box is therefore very important. As plants are seen close up, look for ones with scent, either from flowers or aromatic foliage, and those with a long season of interest so there is always something going on. Wildlife-friendly plants with single, nectar-rich flowers will attract pollinators and provide extra entertainment.

PLANTING TIPS

In the corners at each end of the windowbox use large-leaved, eye-catching plants to accentuate the full length of the box, while airy, light-textured plants towards the middle will mask but not obscure the view from indoors and provide movement and texture. Taller plants in the center will give extra privacy inside — but don't choose plants that are too tall or they will block out light and may get battered by the wind. Trailing plants at the front will tumble over the edge and soften the box outline.

ROOFTOPS

Rooftops are being used increasingly for outdoor living, either as roof gardens or as planting spaces in their own right, and are an ever-popular way of grabbing and greening every available inch of space.

As well as looking beautiful, roof plantings have plenty of environmental benefits. A green roof will insulate the building below as well as help to manage the heat island effect by reducing temperatures and so cut down on energy costs. The planting and soil will help to minimize noise, catch rainwater (and prevent water run-off) and reduce pollution. Green roofs are also an invaluable wildlife habitat, providing food and shelter for insects, invertebrates, and birds.

ROOF GARDENS

Such gardens are often in unique situations, with stunning views and panoramas stretching as far as the eye can see. Always capitalize on this vista, making the most of it when choosing plants, materials, and furniture.

Take inspiration from the scenery around you, and link colors and materials to your surroundings. Use plants to pick out and frame favorite features or mask less attractive sights. They should also be selected so they blend boundaries, creating a seamless flow from your roof to the landscape beyond.

If big enough, roof gardens can have all the features of a garden on the ground. Yet, being up high, there are unique considerations and challenges to bear in mind when planning such an area.

Planning: Before you start always check on whether you need planning permission from your local authority.

Weight: Plants, pots, and soil alone can be a considerable weight, so you need to find out the load-bearing capacity of the structure; this should appear on the title deeds of your home. Otherwise, a structural engineer or architect will be able to advise you on how much weight the roof can take and how it should be distributed.

Drainage: Ensure drainage channels are incorporated into the roof so that water can drain away freely and puddles of water don't collect. Also, keep gutters clear.

Safety: Make sure everything on your roof is firmly secured and that nothing is hanging over the edge. Check with your city or municipality to ensure that your handrail heights are to code. Don't overlook this if you are raising the floor height with tiling or decking.

Access: Think about how you are going to get materials, tools, and plants up onto your roof, and assess the width of stairways and doors. These will dictate your plans as well as the size of plants and materials.

Exposure: Wind, sun, and extremes of temperature are key problems on rooftops, so plants need to be chosen with care. Create shelter with hedging, trellis, and semi-transparent screens, which will slow the wind speed and thereby reduce the impact and damage that high winds can have on plants.

GREEN ROOFS

Roofs, no matter what their size, also offer a brilliant new planting opportunity for what would otherwise be a sterile, barren space. When covered in plants, a green roof will soften and reduce the visual impact of a structure such as a shed or other neighboring building (see pp116–9).

Although green roofs are most commonly used on flat roofs, plants can be grown on gently pitched ones provided the slope is no greater than 20 degrees; if steeper than that, water can run off too easily. Preplanted mats of sedum — shallow-rooting, drought-tolerant plants — are popular. Alternatively, create your own shallow trough on the roof, fill it with soil, and plant with suitable perennials or annuals.

Left: **Up among the chimneys**, roof gardens offer a unique take on the world and almost always have fantastic views that should be embraced and enjoyed.

BALCONIES

Even the tiniest balcony can become a garden in the air (see pp127–9). Although often small and narrow, with little privacy, balconies have views to be embraced and multiple planting opportunities on their floor, walls, and railings or barriers (see pp87–9). Most often seen from inside, they are beautiful garden extensions to a room and give you a uniquely intimate view of the plants you choose to grow.

Every balcony has planting potential but each presents special challenges, which need to be tackled:

Access: Look at the steps and doorways you need to carry plants and materials up and through. They will determine what you can do.

Weight: Balconies are suspended from buildings, and there will be weight restrictions on what you can do, so check its weight-bearing load in your deeds or with a structural engineer before you invest in plants and materials.

Planning permission: Depending on what you want to achieve on your balcony, check whether you require permission from the local authority before you start.

Drainage: Large-scale plantings will need a drainage system to allow water to drain away freely.

Safety: Secure pots and furniture to prevent them from blowing over in high winds and toppling off your balcony to the ground below.

Above: **A mix of plants** including feather grass (*Stipa tenuissima*) and the upright spikes of Russian sage (*Perovskia* "Blue Spire') in this raised balcony bed provides privacy from the world beyond the railings.

Privacy: There is a fine balance between achieving privacy and blocking a view. Use a mix of evergreens, more transparent perennials, and trailing plants that will act as a screen without losing sight of the world beyond.

Growing conditions: Environmental conditions on a balcony can be extreme, with high winds and baking heat causing damage and drought. Other balconies overhead can also cause shade and rain shadows, so choose plants with care.

Above: **Dark, shady patios** can become thriving and attractive growing spaces with the help of light shades of paint on fencing and raised beds and white-flowering plants.

SIDE YARDS

One of the trickiest of spaces for growing plants is the side yard or passage — that narrow pocket of land running along the side of a house. It is often a dark, neglected, dead space, yet it doesn't have to be — especially if it is the only outside space you have.

Side yards are challenging because they are long, thin, and dominated by their boundaries. As these boundaries are often the walls of buildings they therefore block out light, which can lead to problems with damp, particularly in autumn and winter.

Boundaries: These are one of the most dominant features of the side yard so make the most of them. Use them to instill light and interest and allow them to become features all of their own. Fast-growing climbers or a green wall will help the space feel bigger by blurring the boundaries and helping them blend in with their surroundings.

Shade: Use a limited palette of warm, light materials to brighten the space. Create light with mirrors (see pp72–3) and shiny surfaces, and color the walls with paint.

Damp: Shade can cause algae, which will need to be removed regularly to prevent slipping.

Plants: Keep things simple with a few bold species.

BASEMENT PATIOS

Due to their position, basement patios can be cramped, dark, damp and are almost always in full view from above. On the upside, however, they present a gloriously protected growing environment with a unique microclimate. With careful plant choices, these can be special and exciting places for growing.

Access: This can be tricky and the only entry point may well be through the house. Choose simple, low-maintenance plantings so you don't need lots of tools and equipment.

Shade: Lift dank spaces by opting for pale materials for flooring, boundaries, and furniture. Paint or simply wash walls. Use shiny, reflective surfaces to create light (see pp72–3), and look for variegated and white-flowered plants to brighten your space further.

Space: In a confined space keep planting simple, selecting bold, lush, textured foliage over flowers.

A warmer, sheltered environment gives you the opportunity to grow plants that are slightly tender without the need for winter protection, such as tree ferns (*Dicksonia*), palms (*Trachycarpus* or *Chamaerops*), banana plants (*Musa*) and bottlebrush (*Callistemon*). Make the most of it!

Privacy: Small trees can provide a screen from windows higher up, but remember that deciduous trees cast less dense shade than evergreen ones. Or you could add a pergola or arbor for overhead protection, if you have the room. They don't need to be intensely planted, or even at all.

Damp: A lack of light can cause damp conditions and the development of moss and algae on the ground and in beds and containers. You should therefore choose suitable plants and make sure floors are slip resistant. Algae is less obvious on darker floors.

Opposite: **When growing space** is very limited, opt for a few bold plants such as these soft tree ferns (*Dicksonia antarctica*).

THINK OUTSIDE THE BOX

SECTION 3

DESIGN TRICKS

When you're working with a tiny space you need all the help you can get to utilize it in the best way possible and make it look and feel as spacious as you can. Thankfully garden designers have developed lots of neat tricks and creative ways to optimize a space.

Shape: Introducing shapes into your garden is a simple and straightforward way to create the illusion of size. For example, using circles in the design of a square or rectangular plot will make it feel larger because they lead the eye around the space. Similarly, long lines in borders, seating, and water features will lead the eye through the space, accentuating both its length, and width.

Perspective: Playing with perspective cheats the eye and creates the illusion of space. Add height with a tree or arch, or grow climbers against a wall to draw the eye upwards. Rotating the design and layout of your garden by 45 degrees makes it feel much larger, while hiding some of the plot from view triggers intrigue and a sense that there is more to come. A curved path that disappears around a corner, or a cleverly placed pot, offers a tantalizing glimpse of what lies ahead.

Below: **Garden designers** employ clever techniques to trick the eye. This small plot has been designed at an angle to make it feel bigger and suggest a tantalizing view of further space ahead.

Color: One of the most important elements in the garden, color can be used in simple but very effective ways to trick the eye. Different colors create very distinct effects, and when used well, color can make a space feel bigger and brighter than it actually is.

Simplicity: Don't be tempted to use every bit of space. Keep things simple, with a defined, consistent color palette and range of materials, and leave some areas empty so your space can breathe. Group pots together rather and avoid clutter by including built-in seating and clever storage (see pp127–9).

FOCAL POINTS

Focal points are used to add definition to a space. They bring a garden into focus and are particularly invaluable in a small garden, for commanding the eye by directing it to a point that you want emphasized and distracting it from one you don't, such as an unsightly view.

A strong focal point in a garden will provide a feature of interest around which to center the rest of your scheme. The eye naturally follows lines, so placing an accent plant, for example, at the end of a path, in a corner, or by a door works well, although such points can also be positioned at the center of a circular lawn, patio, or bed.

The aim is to make your focal points stand out, so be sure to keep things simple and don't use too many of them. Less is definitely more. Although you could have a number of focal points in a very small space one is probably enough.

Above: **This circular stone pond** nestled in among lush, green foliage is an effective focal point, and its reflective surface and the floating waterlily leaves draw the eye.

The feature also needs to be the right size for its spot and surroundings. Professional designers will achieve this by making sure it meets the criteria of the golden ratio. Essentially this is a ratio of proportion that has been used throughout history to establish a pleasing sense of balance within a space. However in your garden, you will probably be able to establish this size:space ratio purely by eye. If you want to check, mock up the focal point with boxes until you get its size right or, if you already know what feature you're

going to use, experiment by moving it around until it looks right.

As a focal point draws the eye to a particular spot in the garden, make sure that the area around it is worth the extra attention. Look at the background and the planting surrounding it and enhance these if they require it.

An accent point could be seating or a planted pot, sculpture, or water feature. Whatever it is, it must be distinct and not blur with its surroundings.

Seating: An attractive bench or brightly colored chair draws not just the eye but also people physically to an area. Make sure there is an attractive view from the seating.

Plants: Evergreens such as clipped topiary box (*Buxus*) in an attractive planter make great focal points, as do deciduous trees or shrubs, provided they have an interesting shape or bark so even when the leaves are lost they

will command attention. A pot of dazzling bulbs or seasonal bedding can really stand out but will need to be replaced when they fade.

Sculpture: A piece of art is a classic choice for a focal point but you could also use a pretty feature pot or urn. A decorative obelisk will stand out in a bed or border or try a rustic wigwam planted with an evergreen climber.

Water features: A pond or the reflections or movement of a fountain are a striking way to attract attention.

BREAKING UP A SMALL SPACE

One of the classic tricks that designers use to make a space look and feel bigger is to break it up into smaller areas. Not being able to see the whole space in one glance creates intrigue and enhances the illusion of size. The subtle placing of a bench or a plant container that just hides a corner from view is enough to make the eye want to see more and instill the element of surprise.

In a small garden there isn't the space to create separate zones for people to walk through, and it's not possible to block off areas of the garden with solid walls or fences — nor is it necessary. The trick here is to give the illusion that there is something else around the corner by offering the odd glimpse rather than concealing the area from view completely. A low clipped hedge or a row of planted containers is all that is needed to give a hint of what lies beyond, without allowing it to be viewed clearly.

It is enough to imply variety to fool the eye: for example, by a change of surface or paving material, or the placement of a low trellis or a acrylic panel that makes a barrier but still allows light and air in.

Left: **The careful placement** of a brightly colored chair can be enough to lead the eye and encourage people towards a seating area.

Opposite below: **Black fencing** perfectly offsets the silver foliage of the olive tree and the white hydrangea blooms. It also helps to give this small garden a much more spacious feel.

Above: **Using color on boundary** walls and fences can have a huge impact. Here the white slatted fencing brightens this shaded, overlooked garden and helps to instill a feeling of intimacy.

BOUNDARIES

In small spaces, boundaries do so much more than just define the extent of the space. The walls and fences that surround an area are an integral part of its design.

In small gardens, boundaries can easily appear dominant and overwhelming, which in turn makes an area feel small and dark — so don't ignore them. Either disguise or hide your boundaries or embrace them and turn them into a feature.

The right boundary can transform a space. Smothering a wall or fence in plants, either with fast-growing climbers or with vertical features such as pocket planters, will quickly camouflage it and help it to blur and blend in with the world beyond.

Alternatively look at the boundaries you have and see how you can enhance them. Consistency is good — choosing a single, strong style that is carried all the way around will create a feeling of unity and allow you to focus on the garden within rather than being drawn to its boundary.

Replace any old, worn fencing or a fence with a mishmash of different panels, and cover ugly walls with woven screens of willow or bamboo or else paint them.

A boundary painted a light color such as pale gray, cream, or light blue will brighten a dark space, but these colors can also make an area feel smaller as they jump out and grab attention. Dark colors for the boundary such as green, brown, and black will blend in with surrounding plants and make a small space feel bigger.

Painting a feature wall in a different color makes a great design detail and focal point that will help to distract from the size of a space.

COLOR

Color is one of the most powerful elements in a garden. It can influence the way you feel and change how the garden looks. It can be used to set the mood or trick the eye, and it is present not just in every leaf, flower, and stem, but in the walls, paving, and any extra accessories you choose to include.

Professional garden designers know exactly how important color is and how essential it is to get the choice just right. Every color creates a different effect, and the clever use of certain ones can set the tone of a space or change the way that a garden feels entirely.

Dark colors such as black, brown, purple, and deep blue recede and can blur and get lost in the background, which makes them ideal for use as a backdrop in a small space because they will help to make it feel bigger.

Introduce these colors on the boundaries and around the edges of a space, to help it feel larger than it really is.

Vivid, hot colors such as orange, red, and bright yellow are intense and domineering and tend to grab your attention. They are perfect for using on feature walls and for distracting the eye from less attractive sights. However, they can also make a space look smaller if they are used too close to the house or at the front of a border.

Similarly lighter, pastel colors reflect the light and are invaluable in shade. White, pale pink, lemon-yellow, and silver-foliaged plants glow and brighten a gloomy space brilliantly and instill a feeling of calm. But they also jump out at you and can draw the edges in, emphasize boundaries, and make a garden feel small. Use these colors at the front of borders, to lift and brighten other shades and to break up blocks of color.

Opposite: **Color is one** of the most influential design elements in a garden, and the selection of just one strong shade can have the power to change the whole feel and size of a space. Use color on a feature wall either to complement key plants (top left) or to contrast strikingly with them and make them stand out (center right). The color wheel can help you design a planting scheme with colors and shades that work together well (top right, middle, and bottom right) or else experiment with contrasting color schemes for a plant display that makes a real statement (center left and bottom left).

UNDERSTANDING THE COLOR WHEEL

The color wheel is essentially the color spectrum displayed as a circle, and it is helpful for understanding the relationships between colors and how different combinations create a variety of effects. When choosing plants or deciding on furniture remember the following:

- Colors that are next to each other on the wheel look good together and have a pleasing and harmonious effect on the eye.
- Colors that are directly opposite each other (for example, yellow and purple, or red and green) are known as complementary colors and will appear more intense when paired together and produce striking combinations.
- Colors that are an equal distance apart from each other (for example, purple, green, and orange) are known as contrasting colors and work well together in groups of three.

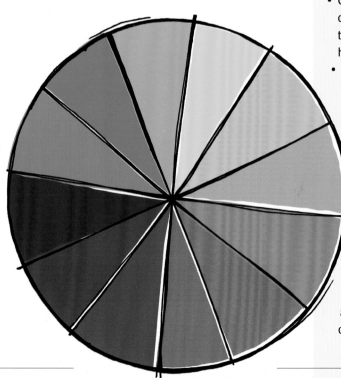

CREATIVE CONTAINERS

Pots and other containers have many practical uses in the garden as well as a distinct design value of their own. With clever positioning and placement they can be used to frame doorways, steps, or vistas, to create a focal point (see p41), or become statement sculptural pieces in their own right.

The style and material of your containers can add color or light to your plot, adding emphasis to the design or brightening a dark space. They can be chosen to match the style of your building, or their shape can be selected to complement and link with the surrounding landscape — a trick that is particularly useful on a rooftop or balcony (see pp96–8).

DESIGN TRICKS WITH POTS

How and where you place your pots can also influence the feel of your gardening space:

- If you place the pots around the edge of a plot, they can make it feel bigger, drawing the eye out to the boundaries; if you move them inwards, they will create a feeling of intimacy and seclusion.
- Group pots together rather than scattering them around. This can help make a space feel spacious and less cluttered.
- Introduce pots to help break up a space into different zones as well as to screen off views or less interesting areas.
- Use pots as an integral part of your design. Repeat the same pots and plants in a row to emphasize or define a boundary or edge (see p82); group smaller planted pots together for greater impact and to create a relaxed oasis of green; or just use the containers on their own — if they are really striking, they won't even need to be planted.

Left: **Pots** make fantastic hanging features, especially when space is limited. Just ensure you use a strong rope and a bracket that will hold their weight.

Right top: **Recycled containers** such as this old zinc bath make great pots and when used creatively can become gorgeous features such as this simple pond filled with waterlilies.

Right center: **Gathering containers** together is a lovely way to display them, and these alpines sunk into a wooden crate form a great centerpiece.

Right below: **Repeating one plant** in rows is a classic design technique, and this stepladder laden with pots of pretty pansies creates a strong focal point.

LIGHTING

Lighting can transform your space. It allows the area to be used after dark, and it can reveal and highlight hidden depths and views that look very different in the daytime. Lighting can also instill a sense of security by surrounding you with a warmly lit, inviting space rather than a black void outside your windows, and it makes the night garden a true outdoor room and extension of your home.

Another advantage of lighting is that it can be functional and help to direct the way around an area, emphasizing steps and pathways and ensuring they are safe. Lighting can also be decorative, highlighting features and focal points and creating atmosphere and ambience. In a small space, lighting is invaluable for creating depth and implying further space, and when used carefully it can become a design element in its own right. Don't overdo it however — the simpler the lighting, the more dramatic the effect.

Clever use of lighting leaves unsightly areas in the dark while spotlights feature trees, plants, and eye-catching vistas. Targeting light at the base of a tree or planter will conjure up beautiful silhouettes and shapes, while lights shone through plants onto the walls behind will bring out magical shadows.

From a practical point of view, lighting can be installed simply by adjusting your existing internal electricity supply. A qualified electrician will ensure that any work is done safely. For a simpler, cheaper, and more ecofriendly effect try tea lights and candles in jars or lanterns placed on a path, or battery-run fairy lights strung among the plants. Braziers and fire bowls also look dramatic while helping you to stay warm, or place solar-powered lights in a sunny spot.

Above left: **Wall lights** such as this nautical-style lantern produce a warm, ambient glow and a pleasant atmosphere for entertaining at night.

Above center: **Tea lights** in pretty lanterns are a cheap and atmospheric way to light your space and a romantic way to guide people around it.

Above right: **Spotlights** are an easy and practical way to make your garden feel safe and secure once daylight fades.

Below left: **Highlighting** favorite plants with spotlights at their base produces enchanting focal points after dark.

Below right: **Position discreet lights** behind plants to create magical shadows on walls and paving.

WATER

Whether it's in a formal fountain, a buzzing wildlife pool, or a simple pond in a pot (see pp109–11), water is a brilliant design tool in any garden. Even the smallest amount will add movement, sound, and a sense of calm. In a confined area, water is particularly invaluable — its ability to introduce light into a space can transform the scene.

A water feature can be as extravagant or as simple as you like. It can be store-bought with a preformed base or be a naturalistic hole in the ground, a recycled barrel, or an old tin bath. In a small garden, water features — whatever their style — make great focal points, and when sited at the end of a path or in a tranquil corner they help to draw the eye and encourage people to peer into their depths.

Round ponds lead the eye around a space while rills (long, narrow channels of water) draw the eye along their length and can help to make a space feel bigger.

Most importantly, still water acts like a mirror, reflecting the sky and the surroundings and is perfect in a small garden for bringing in light, movement, and an ever-changing pattern of color and shape, as clouds move across the sky and the light changes as the day progresses.

Reflections appear their most dramatic on dark water, and this is dependent not on the depth of the pond but on the materials of which

Right: **The water in this low pond** ripples gently, creating movement and light as the reflection of the sky flits across its surface.

it is made. Black dye added to water helps to enhance its depths and sharpen its focus.

When you place your pond, think about reflections, checking them before choosing the pond's final spot. A pond in full sun will reflect the most light but too much sun can cause algae growth. Too shady a site can make the water feel lifeless and dank.

MIRRORS

One of the quickest and easiest ways to make a small space look and feel bigger is to introduce a mirror. When positioned well it is an excellent way to deceive the eye into thinking there is something else beyond the space or that it is part of a much larger garden, while the clever use of reflections creates light and helps to brighten a dingy space throughout the day.

For a mirror to work it has to produce an illusion. The most effective method is to have one that is placed at ground level so that it reflects the bed, path, or pond it is on and continues the feeling of space beyond. Always makes sure that the mirror is showing something worth looking at; the reflection of a bare wall won't fool anyone, so experiment with tilting and angling it until it reveals a border or planted pot. Softening and concealing the edges with climbers and other plants will continue the illusion farther, so that it is not obvious and becomes one with the boundary or wall that it is on (see pp72–3).

Right: **This "antiqued" mirror** forms the boundary in this garden, and cleverly fools the eye so that it is tricky to see where the garden really ends.

Although mirrors are traditionally made of glass, an acrylic one is lighter, safer, and easier to cut; it is also cheaper than glass. Also keep an eye out for "vintage" mirrors in junkyards and second-hand stores. A distressed, mottled, and "antiqued" mirror can be very effective in a small space where unattractive reflections can be a problem — or when you want to avoid looking at your own! The mottling and aged effect can distort and fracture the reflection but still bring light and trick the eye.

The use of mirrors can be controversial — birds can also be fooled and fly into them, although in a small garden, enclosed patio, or side yard this is less likely. Use small expanses of mirror and grow airy plants such as grasses, *Verbena bonariensis*, or *Gaura lindheimeri* in front of them to minimize the risk.

Far left: **Bench seating** that doubles as a storage unit is a clever use of space and a great solution when room is tight.

Left: **Ensuring storage solutions** are practical and sympathetically designed is a must when everything is in full view.

of garden tools and children's toys, keeping them easily accessible while hiding them from view and freeing up precious space.

Use vertical walls for decorative shelving or hang up cupboards for a smaller fit. They can be painted into attractive focal points. When space is really stretched, simply hanging tools on hooks, in a corner or across a wall, can make an attractive and useful feature.

STORAGE

When seeking to maximize your growing space you don't want tools, toys, and equipment cluttering up the area. Therefore almost every outside space needs storage of some kind, and it's important to incorporate it as sympathetically as you can.

Large items such as bikes and bins are best hidden away, and a shed is the easiest way to do this. Unfortunately even a little shed can dominate and overwhelm a small space and become an eyesore. Instead seize the growing opportunity and use the shed as a place for plants — give it a green roof (see pp116–9) or camouflage the sides with climbing plants or vertical planters.

Painting or staining the wood with dark shades of gray, green, blue, even black will help it disappear into the background. Alternatively you could go to the other extreme and turn the shed into a feature by highlighting it with a bright color such as orange or pink.

For smaller items, seating is the easiest and most practical way of providing decent storage without eating into invaluable space. Benches that multitask and double as a trunk with a lift-up seat will hold all manner

SEATING

Seating is essential in every yard. It is the place where we relax, reflect, and entertain, and it is often the spot where we enjoy our green space the most. When used carefully, with a clever choice of style and place, seating can also enhance a design and help to make a space complete.

In a small garden it's important to choose the style and material of your seating carefully. Look for furniture that coordinates with your space and the buildings around it. Too many different styles look cluttered and messy, but a simple color palette and a consistent style will ease the eye, create a sense of coherence, and increase the feeling of space.

Alternatively make the seating emphasize your design or demand attention by turning it into a focal point. A brightly colored or highly stylized chair, strategically placed,

Left: **A storage area** can be transformed into a garden feature with a bountiful green roof.

can lead the eye into a quiet corner or detract from an unsightly view, while integrated benches placed along the edges of your space will help to define its shape and draw the eye out to the edges and corners.

When space is lacking, any features need to multitask. Seating can double up as a storage unit (see opposite). A toolbox can also function as a bench, while a raised bed or a planter can be used as a seat. Simply ensure the ledge is at least 30cm (12in) wide so that it is comfortable to sit.

Carefully placed seating can form inner boundaries or barriers within a space, too, breaking it up into smaller, more intimate areas. Look for seats that have wheels that can be moved around, into the sun or closer to the house, and out of sight when

no longer required, to make a space feel bigger.

If space is really tight, opt for sets that fold up or stack easily so they can be removed completely when not in use, freeing up space.

Top: **A set of foldable bistro furniture** allows you to enjoy outdoor living whenever you like. It can then be stacked away to make the most of the space.

Above: **Bench seating** is a clever way to define a space or to break it up into smaller, more intimate areas. This curved bench forms a private seating area separate from the garden beyond.

VERTICALS

Green Wall Pallet • Succulent Picture Frame • Gutter Planters
Hanging Planted Screen • Pocket Planters • Instant Green Wall
Slatted & Hanging-Chain Screens • Mirror Wall

p.56

p.58

p.64

p.66

GREEN WALL PALLET

There are plenty of DIY wall planters on the market but this recycled pallet is an instant winner for price, ease, and rustic style. When packed with pretty edibles it will also keep you going in fresh leaves, herbs, and vegetables all summer long.

The gaps between the slats in a pallet make perfect pocket planters and mean that your wall planter is almost instantly ready to plant. It just needs to be sealed with plastic around the back and sides to hold the potting mix and plants in place. Most crops like a warm, bright spot so choose a sunny wall for your pallet. Before planting secure it to the wall with eye screws and wire, to stop it from toppling over after watering and when it gets heavy with produce.

Plant the pallet through the slats, treating each row as a separate layer. To help stop potting mix falling through the layers, line each layer with a length of plastic.

We filled a green wall pallet with quick-growing, productive edibles such as lettuces, zucchini, and herbs, but such a pallet could also become a colorful display when planted with bright seasonal plants and annuals.

When using pallets for planting edibles, check to be sure they haven't been chemically treated, so that there is nothing leaching into your food.

Above: **Secured to a sunny wall,** this recycled wooden pallet supports a whole range of edible plants such as herbs, vegetables, and fruit but it could also be planted with a mix of bright annual flowers and trailing leaves.

WHAT YOU WILL NEED

- Tape measure and pencil
- Pallet
- Black plastic sheeting
- Scissors
- Staple gun
- Eye screws or hooks
- Drill and masonry bit
- Wire
- Multipurpose potting mix

PLANTS: A combination of annual edible flowers, herbs, fruit, and vegetables

Edible flowers, like nasturtium, pansy, pot marigold

Herbs, like lemon verbena, rosemary, thyme

Vegetables, like bush tomato, zucchini, snow peas, arugula, lettuce leaves

PLANTING YOUR GREEN WALL PALLET

1 Measure your pallet and cut a sheet of plastic to cover the back and the sides. Use the staple gun to attach it to the pallet.

2 Screw a eye screw or hook into each side of the pallet and position it against the wall. Drill a hole in the wall on either side of the pallet, then screw in an eye screw or hook and fasten it with wire to an eye screw or hook on the pallet.

3 Start to fill the pallet with potting mix, pouring it in from the top until the lowest layer is full.

4 Plant the lowest layer through the slats of the pallet, topping up with potting mix. Then water the layer.

5 Insert a sheet of plastic between this and the layer above it. Continue adding potting mix, planting, watering, and inserting plastic sheeting until you reach the top.

6 Plant the top of the pallet with the more upright plants, such as the tomato and rosemary, and water in.

SUCCULENT PICTURE FRAME

In a small space every inch counts, and these planted picture frames are a beautiful and practical way to green an otherwise drab wall. They are cheap and easy to make and can be scattered across your wall in groups, or used alone as a dramatic, eye-catching statement.

Succulents such as hens and chicks (*Sempervivum*), sedum, and rosularia are perfect for this project — they are some of the easiest plants to grow and tolerant of low moisture and poor or minimal soil. They do need good drainage so use a mix of equal amounts of vermiculite and potting mix. Allow the mix to dry out between waterings.

Once a week in hot, dry weather take each frame down, lay it flat, and water well.

TOP TIP

||||||||||||||||||||||||||||||||||||||||||||||||||||||||||||||||||

Most succulents are easy to split, helping the plants you buy to go even farther. Gently pull clumps apart to make individual plants. These will soon grow, covering an area quickly and giving you more plants for your money.

PLANTING YOUR SUCCULENT PICTURE FRAME

1 Measure the picture frame and then measure and cut your 1 × 2 pieces to make up your planting frame. Screw the frame together. Cut a square of plastic-coated mesh to fit the front of the planting frame and staple it to the frame with the staple gun.

2 Turn the planting frame over and cut a piece of plastic to fit it. Staple the plastic sheet and the original back of the frame (or a piece of cardboard) to the planting frame.

6 As you plant, compress the soil around the succulents with the end of a pencil and top up with more soil so that the plants roots are fully covered. After planting, water well, then leave your picture frame horizontal for a few days, while the plants settle and establish.

7 Attach eye screws to the frame either by inserting one in the center to hook over a nail or by using two eyes — one on either side connected by wire — and hang your frame from this.

3 Mix together equal amounts of soil and vermiculite and feed it carefully through the mesh until the frame is full. Don't firm it down yet, as you need to leave room for the plants.

4 Using a drill and self-drilling screws, attach the picture frame to the planting frame.

5 Plant through the mesh by cutting small gaps with the pliers, wire cutters, or scissors, but snip only as much as you need. The wires are there to hold the plants securely in the frame.

Below: **Succulents such as hens and chicks and stonecrop** come in a variety of leaf colors, shapes, and textures, making this pretty succulent picture frame a work of art.

WHAT YOU WILL NEED

- Tape measure and pencil
- Picture frames (ours were a mix of second-hand and discount-store buys)
- Lengths of 1 × 2 (25 × 50mm)
- Wood saw
- Drill, masonry bit, and self-tapping screws
- Plastic-coated mesh
- Pliers, wire cutters, or scissors
- Staple gun
- Old plastic potting mix bag
- Multipurpose potting mix and perlite
- Eye screws

PLANTS: Succulents, e.g. *Crassula* "Tresco Seaspray," *Echeveria elegans*, *Pachyphytum* "Dark Red," *Rosularia sedoides*, *Sedum acre* "Aureum," *S. rupestre*, *S. spathulifolium* "Purpureum"

GUTTER PLANTERS

Gutters are a cheap, easy, and effective way to clothe an unsightly wall or fence. As planters they can be any size, grouped in rows or dotted across a wall. They look great planted with anything from flowering perennials to simple alpines.

Gutters can be used in place of seed trays. In this project, the lengths of functional plastic become cheap, simple-to-make planters. Choose large gutters so that plants have enough soil. Your gutters can be cut to any length and used in any combination.

Gutter planters are simple to put together, with end stops to hold the potting mix conveniently in place (you could tape up the ends with duct tape but it's not so neat). There are also brackets to secure the gutters to a wall.

Any quick-growing annuals or shallow-rooting perennials will be happy in these planters, while edibles such as strawberries, lettuce leaves, and herbs will also thrive.

Planting with a single ornamental species, such as the Mexican fleabane (*Erigeron karvinskianus*) we've used, looks particularly dramatic, but any mix of vibrant seasonal bedding plants would provide a changeable and colorful display. Alpines such as *sedum* and *sempervivum*, topdressed with pea gravel, also make a striking, contemporary, year-round display.

Use multipurpose potting mix here, rather than a heavier, soil-based one, and mix with vermiculite or perlite to aid drainage. Holes drilled through the bottom of the gutters will also help drainage.

PLANTING YOUR GUTTERS

1 Measure your length of gutter and cut it to size with a saw. Hold the brackets up against the wall and mark where they are to go; use the level to ensure they are level. Drill the pilot holes through the brackets. Attach the brackets to the wall using anchors and screws.

2 Clip the gutters into the brackets and use the drill to make evenly spaced drainage holes along its length.

3 Attach the end stops to the gutters, or seal the ends with duct tape. Then fill the gutters with a mix of three parts potting mix to one part pea gravel, leaving enough space for planting.

A: Topdress alpines and succulents with pea gravel to keep moisture away from the leaves. Treated in this way, they will thrive in the shallow soil of the gutter.

B: Filling gutters with just one long-flowering ornamental such as this Mexican fleabane gives a striking designer look.

C: Arugula, mustard, oriental (Asian) leaves, and cut-and-come-again salad mixes can all be sown, every couple of weeks, across the gutters for regular pickings of fresh green leaves.

4 Plant up, adding potting mix and firming down as you go. Then water the plants in well, to help them establish.

WHAT YOU WILL NEED

- Tape measure and pencil
- Lengths of PVC gutters (we used 112mm/4½ in half rounds)
- Jigsaw
- Gutter brackets
- Level
- Drill, masonry bit, wood drill bit, anchors, and screws
- End stops or duct tape
- Multipurpose potting mix
- Vermiculite or perlite (you can use horticultural pea gravel instead but be aware that this will be heavier)

PLANTS:

A *Sedum spathulifolium* "Cape Blanco," *Sempervivum*, *Thymus pseudolanuginosus*

B *Erigeron karvinskianus*

C Cut-and-come-again lettuce seeds or plug plants, e.g. romaine, oak leaf lettuce, mizuna, mustard greens, arugula

HANGING PLANTED SCREEN

A screen is perfect for a balcony or anywhere you need a bit of privacy yet still want to let in light and have a partial view. Planted with trailing plants, a screen can also be used to break up and hide a space.

Our screen had just three levels but it can have more or less depending on your needs, and be as long as the gutters will allow — simply cut it to fit your space. We have also used only one screen but you could hang three or four together to define or hide your area.

The levels are created by threading the gutters onto two lengths of rope at each end (doubling up ensures the gutter is balanced and level). The rope is measured as you go to make sure that you have an equal length between each level of gutter and also to check there is enough room for the plants between each one. End stops for the gutters help to keep the potting mix in place, and drainage holes drilled

Above: **Trailing evergreens** such as ivy help to provide privacy in this planted screen while the purple pansies offer a flash of cheery color.

through the gutter base allow water to flow freely through and prevent plants from getting too wet.

The plants you use will depend on the amount of seclusion you require. Densely leaved and trailing plants will block out your surroundings effectively but will also let less light through. A more transparent planting will provide tantalizing glimpses of the view beyond.

PLANTING YOUR HANGING PLANTED SCREEN

1 Measure and cut your pieces of gutter into equal sizes. Work out and mark where the two rope holes are going at each end of the various pieces of gutter. Attach the gutter end stops.

2 Drill the holes for the ropes at the ends of each gutter. Then make evenly spaced drainage holes along the length of each piece of gutter. Cut the rope into four equal-length pieces.

3 Thread one length of rope through a hole in the first piece of gutter and tie a knot underneath, for the gutter to rest on. Then thread the remaining lengths through the other holes in that piece. Measure along the lengths of rope marking exactly where you want the next piece of gutter to rest.

WHAT YOU WILL NEED

- Tape measure and pencil
- Lengths of PVC gutter (we used 112 mm/4½ in half rounds) plus end stops
- Jigsaw
- Drill bit
- Sisal rope, 8mm (⅓in) (we left about 30cm, 1ft, between each tier so each rope length was at least 1.2m, 4ft, and there were four pieces of this length)
- Hooks for hanging
- Multipurpose potting mix

PLANTS: Ivy, *Nepeta* "Grannilocks," pansy

4 Tie a knot over each mark and then thread the next level of gutter through the ropes, pushing it securely onto each knot. Continue this process until all the levels of gutter are secured to the ropes. At each end tie the two ropes together at the top so that the screen is ready for hanging.

5 Screw hooks or brackets onto wherever you wish to hang your screen and position it. Fill each level with potting mix and plant, starting at the top so that it doesn't fall onto the plants below. Water the plants in well.

POCKET PLANTERS

These ready-to-hang pocket planters are an easy way to grow the plants you love, from juicy strawberries or bright annuals to stylish succulents. Simply plant, hang, and enjoy.

Ready-made hanging pocket planters are available in a whole range of materials and colors, from plastic to recycled fabric, in the brightest red to the plainest black. For a striking look choose dark colors — the planters will disappear into the background leaving just the plants to stand out. Alternatively, opt for brighter hues to complement or clash dramatically with your choice of planting.

Use a multipurpose potting mix, rather than a heavier, soil-based one, and mix in slow-release fertilizer and water-retaining gel to help keep your plants fed and moist. Don't be tempted to overplant the pockets; if you do so, your plants will struggle and you'll spend all your time watering and feeding.

If you think you will need to take the pockets down regularly to replant or water, hang them with cup hooks rather than screwing them to the wall.

Many different plants will tolerate pocket life including perennials such as ferns, heuchera, geranium, and small grasses.

Our alpine pockets contained a mix of glaucous-leaved and purple-hued *sempervivum*, sedum, and other drought-loving, hardy succulents, which will thrive in such conditions.

Strawberries are more than happy growing in shallow planters, so we inserted two plants per pocket. We used the pink-flowered "Toscana," which not only matches the planter perfectly but also provides a flash of color even before the fruit appears.

WHAT YOU WILL NEED

- Vertical pocket planters
- Drill, masonry bit, and screws or cup hooks
- Slow-release fertilizer and water-retaining gel
- Multipurpose potting mix
- Horticultural pea gravel to topdress the alpines

PLANTS: Small annuals and perennials, e.g. strawberry plants, alpines, salads, seasonal bedding

TOP TIP

Lots of plants thrive in pockets. For different looks you could try:
Scented: Lavender, rosemary, scented-leaf pelargonium, thyme
Evergreen: Bugle (*Ajuga*), carex, geranium, heather, heuchera, tea tree (*Leptospermum*)
Spring and summer flowers: Bidens, fleabane (*Erigeron*), fuchsia, lantana, nasturtium
Autumn and winter flowers: Cyclamen, pansy, primrose, solanum, wallflowers

Opposite **A:** Hardy succulents enjoy a fairly dry, free-draining soil, making them perfect for pocket planters. Mix trailing types and rosettes for a dramatic look.
B: Grow two strawberry plants per pocket. Choose early, mid-, and late-season varieties for a longer fruit harvest.

PLANTING YOUR POCKET PLANTERS

1 Using a drill, fasten the pocket planter to the wall or fence with screws or cup hooks.

2 Add slow-release fertilizer and water-retaining gel to the potting mix, to provide plants with extra food and to reduce the need for watering. You do not need water-retaining gel for alpines.

3 Pour the mix into each pocket, filling them two-thirds full.

4 Plant into the pockets starting with the one at the top, so that the potting mix won't fall onto the plants below. Water the plants in well. Topdress alpines with pea gravel.

INSTANT GREEN WALL

Extend your growing space and transform the walls around you with a simple, store-bought wall kit. When filled with lush ferns, colorful heucheras, and bright grasses it's just the thing to lift a shady spot.

Even though green walls have long been a fashion statement, they are still an exciting and effective way to gain extra growing space in a tight spot. There are numerous easy-to-erect kits on the market, so choose whichever is best for you and your space. Always look for planters that provide large, deep pockets — the more growing room plants have, the less time you spend feeding and watering. Kits could also include an irrigation device, for cutting down on watering even more.

Use a lightweight drainage material. Opt for a soil-based potting mix for long-term living walls, and a multipurpose one for short-term displays.

This planter is on a shady wall, and its plants are ideal for a balcony or urban plot where nearby walls can cast almost constant shade. If sun does shine on your plot, add fuchsia and geranium for a splash of extra color. Arrange your plants as naturally as you can, using different foliage types to make waves through the planter, and dot through flowering or fruiting plants such as lilyturf (*Liriope*) to add color.

Above: **It may measure just 1 × 1m (3 × 3ft),** but this brilliant wall planter packed with bold, lush plants draws the eye beautifully.

WHAT YOU WILL NEED

- Living Wall kit (we used a 1 × 1m/3 × 3ft one)
- Level
- Pencil
- Drill, masonry bit, anchors, screws, and washers
- Lightweight drainage material, e.g. clay aggregate
- Multipurpose potting mix

PLANTS:

Asplenium scolopendrium, Bergenia cordifolia, Carex oshimensis "Evergold," *Dryopteris affinis* "Cristata," *D. erythrosora, Heuchera* "Melting Fire," *Liriope muscari* "Moneymaker"

PLANTING YOUR INSTANT GREEN WALL

1 Position your planter and make sure it is straight by placing a level on the top. Mark where the screws need to go and drill the holes. Insert the anchors, then fix your planter to the wall with the screws and washers, making sure it is secure and firm.

2 Once the planter is up, fill each of the pockets with the drainage material, pouring it in until you have a 5–6cm (2–2½in) layer at the bottom. Use your fingers to make sure the layer is spread evenly across each pocket.

3 Top up each pocket with a layer of potting mix, filling it only about two-thirds full so that there is still enough room for the plants. Remove the plants from their pots and start to arrange them in the planter.

4 Place the plants in each pocket in as natural a pattern as possible. The best way to do this is to plant in drifts and blocks, using the more textural foliage plants such as ferns in narrow swathes and arranging the broader-leaved plants in bold blocks of color.

5 When you are happy with the way the plants look, fill in around each one with more potting mix. Firm in as you go, to get rid of any air pockets. Top up with potting mix to about 3cm (1¼in) below the rim of each pocket, to allow space for watering.

6 Water your new plants in well and continue to keep them well watered until they are established. Multipurpose potting mix contains enough nutrients to help your plants settle in, but after six weeks and then throughout the rest of the growing season give them a regular boost with a general-purpose feed.

SLATTED & HANGING-CHAIN SCREENS

Even the smallest space can fit a screen. As well as being perfect for hiding or masking a view or part of the garden, it can also be introduced to divide up a space and create a smaller, more intimate area within.

Here we show you how to make two screens: one solid, for hiding or defining an area; and one that uses plants to create an airy, more transparent divide.

Both screens are based around a simple wood frame that can be made to any size, according to your needs. Paint it to blend in with its surroundings or to stand out and make a statement.

Our frame was screwed to the adjacent fence post and then attached to the paving with ground anchor bolts. However you could also concrete the upright posts of the frame directly into the ground for extra stability if your screen is to be used across a bed or border.

Our slatted screen had 19 × 32mm (¾ × 1¼in) cedar slats nailed across it to create a solid barrier. The width of the gap between the slats is adjustable and will depend on how much privacy you want and how much light you wish to let in.

We used the side of one of the wood slats to establish the gap

A

between the slats. This ensured we had an even space between each one while allowing some light to permeate. However you could have 10mm (½in) for a thinner gap or 38mm (1½in) for a wider one.

The hanging-chain screen, which had lengths of chain hung on the

frame, was intended for use above a planter so that plants are able to climb up the chain to make a lighter, living screen. The chains can be hung at any distance apart, but just make sure you don't overcrowd the planting. The plants must always have enough room in which to grow.

WHAT YOU WILL NEED

- Tape measure and pencil
- 4 × lengths of pressure-treated wood, 50 × 50mm (2 × 2in), for the screen frame
- Wood saw
- Drill, masonry bit, and self-tapping screws
- Exterior wood stain or paint and paintbrush
- Ground anchor bolts, for attaching the frame to the ground

A CHAIN SCREEN

- Galvanized chain
- Heavy-duty, screw-in hooks

B SLATTED SCREEN

- Lengths of pressure-treated wood, 50 × 50mm (2 × 2in), for the slats
- Hammer and stainless steel nails or lost head (countersunk) screws, to fix the wood slats

TOP TIP

To save time, saw two pieces of wood together if they are to be of equal length. If you don't have the space to cut it yourself, get your local wood yard or DIY store to do it for you.

Opposite: **This bright, large-flowered Clematis "Remembrance"** is perfect for this chain screen but any fast-growing climber would work. For year-round cover opt for evergreens such as *Clematis armandii* or confederate jasmine (*Trachelospermum jasminoides*).

MAKING YOUR SCREEN FRAME

1 Measure the area to be covered by your screen. Then measure and saw off the 2 × 2 pieces for its frame.

2 Drill and fasten the four frame pieces together with self-tapping screws. Paint with wood stain or paint.

3 Attach your frame to the ground with the anchor bolts and to the supporting fence with the screws.

MAKING YOUR HANGING-CHAIN SCREEN

1 Measure and mark out where each of the chains is to hang along the top of your screen frame, making sure that they are regularly spaced.

2 Insert the hooks by drilling their holes and then screwing them in.

3 Hang a chain from each hook and either trim its base or leave overlong. The plants grown at the base will soon cover any excess chain.

MAKING YOUR SLATTED SCREEN

1 Cut each slat to fit the width of your screen frame. Fasten the first slat by nailing both ends to the screen frame.

2 To ensure an even gap between each slat, turn one upright to expose its depth, then place and hold it between the first slat and the second one.

3 Nail the second slat to the screen frame and continue to attach the rest of the slats in the same way, holding an upright slat between each one to ensure they are evenly spaced.

Opposite: **A slatted screen** is a great way to break up an area without blocking out too much light. With climbing plants such as this *Trachelospermum jasminoides* scrambling up it, a screen like this will add an extra vertical green feature to your growing space.

MIRROR WALL

Mirrors are a classic way to make a small space look larger, and this simple project does just that. The mirror is set within a frame that has been painted to help it disappear into the background, and it beautifully reflects the garden beyond and successfully creates the illusion that the garden is bigger than it really is. You can use any size or shape of mirror — just pick whatever suits your space.

Mirrors can be left fully exposed and clearly seen within the garden, like ours, or be slightly hidden by plants so that they really trick the eye.

We used an acrylic mirror, a great alternative to traditional glass, as it is cheaper, lighter to transport, and easy to cut to size, and there is no need to worry about breaks and shattered glass. Another tip is to keep an eye out for second-hand mirrors. In a small space, where it can be difficult to avoid your own reflection, introducing tarnished, mottled mirrors is a great trick — the patina reduces the reflection and makes the mirror less distracting.

Try placing the mirror in a number of spots in the garden before putting it up. Different angles will provide a variety of reflections, so it's worth making sure you get it right.

MAKING YOUR MIRROR WALL

1 Turn your mirror face down and measure its width and length.

2 Measure and cut the trim to make a frame. Then screw the pieces together.

WHAT YOU WILL NEED

- Acrylic mirror
- Tape measure and pencil
- Lengths of pressure-treated wood, 19 × 38mm (¾ × 1½in)
- Wood saw
- Drill, wood bit, masonry bit (if attaching to a wall), and screws
- Exterior wood stain or paint and paintbrush
- Mirror glue
- Level

4 Apply an even amount of glue to the back of your mirror and stick it carefully to the frame.

3 If you want to, stain or paint your frame so that it will blend into the background when it is hung.

5 Use a level to ensure your mirror is straight when you attach it to your wall or fence with the appropriate screws.

Above: **Many designers are fond of using mirrors** to make a space look bigger. When placed well they will also bring light and color because they cleverly reflect the sky and plants around them.

HANGING & HIGHRISE

Shady Hanging Basket • Hanging Herbs
Triple Hanging Baskets • Pots on Hooks • Potted Shelves
Balcony Rail Planters

p.80

p.87

SHADY HANGING BASKET

When you're short of space, hanging baskets are a great solution. This sophisticated, evergreen basket is perfect for a shady spot, being crammed full of ferns and other shade-loving plants that will thrive in the darkest of corners.

We chose a woven coir liner for our hanging basket (if using a more traditional sphagnum moss one, ensure it is from a sustainable source), and we then sprayed the outside of the liner black to help the plants really stand out.

When planting, it can help to prop the hanging basket in a large plant pot to keep it steady, then place the liner in the basket. Add a circle of plastic, cut from an old potting mix bag, to the liner base to help hold in water, before filling with potting mix.

Soilless potting mix is best in a hanging basket because a soil-based one gets very heavy when wet. For perennial plants, which will be in the basket for a long time, it is a good idea to mix in some slow-release fertilizer when planting. If you think watering may be a problem, add water-retaining gel to the potting mix to help store moisture.

Right: **Lift a gloomy,** shady spot with a lush green hanging basket. Filled with compact ferns and other evergreens, it provides year-round color and interest.

PLANTING YOUR SHADY HANGING BASKET

1 Use spray paint to cover the outside of the coir liner, applying a few extra coats to make sure there is an even covering. Wear rubber gloves if you want to protect your hands.

2 When the liner is dry, place it in the basket. Cut a disc of black plastic from an old potting mix bag for the base and place inside the liner.

3 Half-fill the basket with potting mix and add in slow-release fertilizer and water-retaining gel.

WHAT YOU WILL NEED

- Large hanging basket, 40cm (16in) in diameter
- Woven coir liner
- Black spray paint
- Old plastic potting mix bag
- Scissors
- Soilless potting mix
- Slow-release fertilizer and water-retaining gel
- Hanging basket bracket or hooks for hanging

PLANTS: *Athyrium filix-femina*, *Dryopteris erythrosora*, *Heuchera* "Midnight Rose," *Pellaea rotundifolia*

4 Arrange the plants in the basket until you are happy with the way they look. Then plant, filling in with potting mix as you go.

5 Hang your basket from a bracket or hook attached to the wall or fence, making sure it is at a safe height. Then water well.

HANGING HERBS

Transforming a collection of rustic clay pots filled with herbs into a charming hanging garden is a great way to grow and display these useful plants. Whether on a balcony or outside the kitchen door, these hanging herbs will provide you with fresh, healthy leaves whenever you need them.

Our pretty pots were strung with rope for hanging. Put some masking tape on the rim of each pot, to stop the clay cracking and the drill from slipping, before you make the three holes for the ropes. Each rope is threaded though each hole twice, for extra stability, so loop it before threading, so that you have a piece of double thickness. Once you have threaded the rope through all three holes, tie all the lengths together at the top to make a strong hanger that can be looped over a hook or nail.

Pots of different sizes and shapes look best, while hanging them at various heights will give the most interesting and varied display. Just

Above: **These easy-to-make** hanging planters are a great way to grow herbs or other Mediterranean-style plants, such as lavender or trailing pelargoniums.

make sure they are at a height that is comfortable for picking but not a danger to passers-by.

Harvest the herbs regularly, picking leaves from across the plant so that regrowth is even and your plants stay in good shape.

Most of the herbs we used grow best in sun. If your space is shady try parsley, coriander (cilantro), chervil, chives, mint, or oregano instead.

PLANTING YOUR HANGING HERBS

1 To work out where the ropes are to go, measure the rim of each pot, divide the circumference by three, and then make a mark for each of the three equally spaced holes. Stick a piece of masking tape over each spot. Carefully drill the holes and then remove the tape.

2 Loop a length of rope or twine and pull it through a hole until you have a double piece of equal length on either side. Do this for each hole.

3 Gather all the lengths of rope together and trim off the ends with scissors so that they are even. Then knot them securely together.

WHAT YOU WILL NEED

- Tape measure and pencil
- Recycled terracotta pots of different sizes and shapes
- Masking tape
- Drill and twist drill bit
- Rope or twine
- Scissors
- Gravel for drainage material and topdressing
- Multipurpose potting mix
- S-shaped hooks or eye screws

PLANTS: Herbs, e.g. basil, mint, oregano, rosemary, thyme

4 Put a layer of drainage material in the base of each pot and add some potting mix.

5 Plant, topdress, and hang each herb pot onto an S-shaped hook or eye screw. Keep an eye on the condition of the rope or twine as it is likely to rot over time and may need replacing.

TRIPLE HANGING BASKETS

A multilayered display such as this stunning hanging garden is just the thing when growing in the ground is limited or impossible. Each of the baskets could be planted with one bold species, bringing either color, height, or flowers to the display, or else be filled with a variety of trailing plants or brightly colored annuals.

To help you establish the right levels and distances between the three baskets, this project is best made and planted *in situ*. The baskets are hung on lengths of galvanized chain, and the links are used to help you set all the baskets at the same height. The distance between them should be equal, yet also depend on the height of the plants. Make sure they have enough room to grow, so try the tallest plants in the baskets to check, before attaching to the chain.

Secure the baskets to the chain with cable ties, doubling up the ties if you are worried about stability. Then line the base with a disc of plastic cut from an old potting mix bag, to stop water flooding the plants below. A lighter, multipurpose or soilless potting mix is better than a soil-based one, which can get very heavy when wet.

For simplicity and effect we used just one type of plant in each basket, but you could have a mix or the same plant throughout.

Above: **Three tiers of plants** make up this stunning display. A creative take on the traditional hanging basket, it is a great solution when there is limited space in the ground.

WHAT YOU WILL NEED

- 3 × hanging baskets of decreasing size, e.g. 35cm (14in), 40cm (16in), 45cm (18in)
- 3 × matching woven coir or sisal liners
- Lengths of galvanized chain
- Hanging basket bracket or hook
- Cable ties and scissors
- Metal cutters
- Old plastic potting mix bag
- Multipurpose or soilless potting mix, water-retaining gel, and slow-release fertilizer

PLANTS:

Top basket: *Carex oshimensis* "Everest"

Middle basket: *Persicaria bistorta* "Superba"

Bottom basket: *Imperata cylindrica* "Rubra"

PLANTING YOUR TRIPLE HANGING BASKETS

1 Place each coir or sisal liner into its appropriately sized basket. Hang your three chains from the same bracket or hook, and then remove the original chain from each basket. Decide where the smallest basket is to go by counting the chain links to help you.

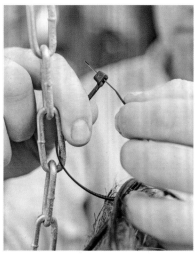

2 Attach the rim of the smallest basket to each chain with cable ties, making sure that the chains are evenly spaced around the basket.

3 Hang the medium-sized and largest baskets, ensuring that you have given your chosen plants enough room to grow.

4 Trim all the excess lengths of cable ties and check the baskets are hanging straight and securely. Cut off any excess chain with metal cutters.

5 Cut a disc of plastic for the base of each liner and place in position. Half-fill the smallest basket with potting mix combined with water-retaining gel and fertilizer. Plant this basket first — by starting with the one at the top you prevent the potting mix from dirtying plants below.

6 Add potting mix to the medium-sized basket and plant it up. Repeat for the largest basket. To complete your hanging garden, water all the plants in well.

POTS ON HOOKS

Pots and other containers no longer need be left solely down on the ground. With the help of simple butcher's hooks you can transform any fence or wall into a beautiful hanging garden.

The more pots you use for this project the better and the greener your space will become. They can be displayed in regular rows or grids or be hung randomly across the wall or fence.

We painted new terracotta pots for this project, but you could use any pots or other containers, even recycled tin cans. Whichever material you choose, apply masking tape over the spot where each hole is to be drilled, to stop the drill slipping and to prevent your container cracking. Remember to drill drainage holes in the base if your pot doesn't have them.

Butcher's S-shaped hooks are readily available from kitchen shops and DIY stores and are perfect for just hooking over trellis. Alternatively you can string wire tautly between eye screws and hang your pots on this. Use tension hooks at each end of the wire to help keep the wire tight and prevent it from sagging under the weight of the pots.

Spraying the pots with paint transforms plain clay pots into colorful, glazed-effect containers that will go perfectly with your color scheme. Paint also has the added benefit of making clay less porous, which helps to cut down on the need to water.

We used the same plant — *Angelonia* Angelface Blue — in all our pots to direct the eye along the fence but any bright seasonal bedding would look lovely. Try heuchera, tiarella, or ferns for year-round cover. Climbing plants such as ivy

Above: **S-shaped hooks** slipped through holes drilled in the pot rims allow you to green a fence or trellis quickly and easily.

or *Clematis armandii* would trail beautifully and give more of a green wall look.

WHAT YOU WILL NEED

- Masking tape and pen
- Plain terracotta pots
- Drill and masonry bit
- Spray paint and rubber gloves
- Old plastic potting mix bag and scissors
- Multipurpose potting mix and general fertilizer
- S-shaped hooks

PLANTS: *Angelonia,* Angelface Blue

PLANTING YOUR POTS ON HOOKS

1 Use a strip of masking tape to mark where each hole is to go on each pot. The masking tape will help to stop the drill bit from slipping and will also prevent the terra cotta from cracking. A hole through the rim will give the best support.

2 With the pot placed upside down on a flat surface, carefully drill a hole through each pot rim.

3 Put on protective gloves, then spray the pots with your chosen color. A few light layers will give a smoother, more even finish than trying to cover the pot in one pass.

4 Cut a small disc of plastic from an old potting mix bag for the bottom of each pot. Half-fill each pot with potting mix and add a sprinkle of general fertilizer.

5 Plant up each pot, fill in with more potting mix, and firm down. Slip an S-shaped hook through the hole of each pot, hang them up, and water the plants in well.

POTTED SHELVES

Shelves are an increasingly popular way to display pots in the garden, and this project brings the concept bang up to date — without the need for endless drilling and brackets. These rope-hung shelves can be used to cover a wall or be left free-standing to divide or screen a space.

Our hanging shelves had three tiers holding three pots in each, but the boards could be made longer to hold more pots or there could be more tiers — whatever suits the space you want

to "green."

Once you have worked out the position of each pot, use a circle drill bit to make the pot holes. String the shelves together with two lengths of rope at each end, to ensure they are balanced.

To make sure that the distance between the shelves is equal and that there is enough light and space for the plants to develop between them, carefully measure and mark on each rope where each shelf is to go. The ropes are knotted below each shelf and then gathered together at the top and knotted again before being hung from hooks.

For our shelves we selected our favorite mix of herbs, but any potted plants could be used to match your

planting scheme.

Opposite: **These hanging shelves** will green a wall or provide a screen to achieve privacy or intimacy. The simple terracotta pots complement the herbs well but they could also be painted for extra color.

TOP TIP

To establish the position of three pots along a shelf we measured the length of the board and divided it by four. We then measured the width of the board and halved that figure, to ensure each pot was exactly in the center of the board and equally spaced along it.

WHAT YOU WILL NEED

- Tape measure and pencil
- 9 × plain terracotta pots
- 3 × wood boards of equal length
- Drill and circle bits to match the diameter of your pots
- Sisal rope, 8mm (⅓in) in diameter (we left about 40cm, 16in, between each tier so each rope length was at least 1.6m, 5¼ft, and there were 4 pieces of this length)
- Hooks for hanging

PLANTS: Mint, arugula, thyme, rosemary, sage, strawberry

PLANTING YOUR POTTED SHELVES

1 Measure and mark where each pot is going along each board.

2 Use a circle bit on your drill to make the holes for the pots on each board. Discard the excess wood.

continued overleaf ...

continued …

3 Drill the two holes for the ropes at each end of each board. Thread the rope through what will be the bottom shelf, securing it with knots underneath.

4 Lay out the remaining boards and measure the space between each one so that you have an equal height between the shelves and enough room for the plants to flourish. Clearly mark the shelf positions on the ropes.

5 Knot each rope at a marked spot before threading it through the next shelf.

6 Repeat this for the other holes and shelves. Then tie all the ropes together at the top, and hang the shelves over your hooks.

7 Once the shelves are secure, place each planted pot into a hole.

ALTERNATIVE PLANTS TO USE

Look for plants that either flower or have year-round leaf color and will spill over and soften the edge of the pots.

Trailing flowering plants, e.g. aubrieta, bidens, *Campanula poscharskyana*, osteospermum, pelargonium, petunia

Trailing evergreen plants, e.g. bugle (*Ajuga*), × *Heucherella* "Redstone Falls," × *H.* "Yellowstone Falls," ivy, persicaria, *Rosmarinus officinalis* Prostratus Group, *Stachys byzantina* "Silver Carpet," *Vinca minor*

BALCONY RAIL PLANTERS

This inspired project puts popular pocket planters to new use, transforming them into clever but simple balcony saddlebags. When straddling a fence or railings they bring color to each side — for you and your neighbors to enjoy.

There are many different types of pocket planters available to buy. For this project, where exposure to wind was likely to be a problem, we opted for the more rigid, plastic or canvas types. Two were secured together by threading cable ties through the holes at the top, which would normally be used to hang them on a wall. (If your pocket planters don't have holes, simply make some with a screwdriver and use masking tape around each hole to strengthen it.)

For ease, plant the pocket planters before hanging. Fill them with multipurpose potting mix combined with slow-release fertilizer and water-retaining gel, which will help cut down on feeding and watering in such a comparatively small space. Once the saddlebags are planted up and in position, use more cable ties to secure them halfway down and at the bottom, to protect them from strong winds.

The saddlebags will provide good cover as well as color on your balcony. Adjust the number you introduce and the size of the gap between them according to the amount of privacy and shelter you want. Fill with a mix of

PLANTING YOUR BALCONY RAIL PLANTERS

1 Lay the pocket planters flat on the ground with their top ends together and secure them in adjacent corners with cable ties to make one saddlebag set. Trim off loose ends with scissors or pliers.

2 While the planters are still on the ground fill each pocket with potting mix mixed with water-retaining gel and slow-release fertilizer. Then plant in each pocket.

WHAT YOU WILL NEED

- 2 × pocket planters per basket set
- Cable ties and strong scissors or pliers
- Multipurpose potting mix, water-retaining gel, and slow-release fertilizer

PLANTS: Annual and seasonal perennials including trailing foliage and flowering types (we used bacopa, campanula, ivy, and petunia)

3 Carefully hang your saddlebag set by lowering it over the railings with one pocket planter on each side. Secure with cable ties in the middle and at the base, to stop it being caught by the wind.

bright, cheery perennials or annuals and trailing plants for instant impact.

Above left: **These ingenious planters** fixed to scaffolding poles make a wonderful green screen for people to enjoy from both sides.

Above right: **Undemanding succulents** bring year-round color to a balcony and will thrive in the inhospitable conditions found there.

Left: **A windowbox** full of chives, thyme, and other culinary herbs is both productive and attractive.

Opposite: **Pocket planters** are simply strung together with cable ties to produce these brilliant displays. When slung over railings or fencing, purple campanula and petunia, bright bacopa, and trailing ivy cleverly bring color to both sides of the railings.

POTS & PLANTERS

p.92

p.94

p.102

p.106

p.96

p.99

p.109

Above: **Each of these pots** contains a mix of multi seasonal plants that will bring color and interest from spring right through to the dark days of winter.

POTS FOR YEAR-ROUND INTEREST

When space is at a premium, selecting the right plants is key, and those that provide color and interest for more than one season are always a wise choice. These three pots contain a variety of perennials, annuals, and bulbs that will produce something of interest for your garden every week of the year.

It is worth giving your choice of pots careful consideration. These should be something you will want to look at for months to come. We settled on a group of pots that were all in the same style.

If your pots don't have drainage holes, drill some in the base. Include a layer of drainage material such as clay aggregate, styrofoam chips, tufa, or broken pottery to allow water to flow freely from the pot; old plastic plant pots are particularly good in large pots.

Use a soil-based potting mix, because the majority of your plants will be in their container for a long time. You should add in slow-release fertilizer with the potting mix to help give plants a boost.

There are plenty of plants that are more than mere one-hit wonders, and they offer color and value throughout the year. To guarantee constant interest you should have at least one of them as the backbone of each pot. Add to this a mix of seasonal bulbs and annuals that can be changed as they fade and your pots will bring a smile year-round.

PLANTING YOUR POTS FOR YEAR-ROUND INTEREST

1 Use a drill to make drainage holes in the base of each pot. You can use masking tape to help prevent the drill from slipping.

2 Pour a generous layer of drainage material into each pot. Add potting mix combined with slow-release fertilizer until the pot is about two-thirds full — you need to leave enough room for the biggest plant to be at the right planting depth.

3 Arrange your plants in each pot until you are happy with the way they look. Then plant them, making sure each rootball is at or just below the surface of the potting mix. Top up with more potting mix and water the plants in well.

WHAT YOU WILL NEED

- Drill and drill bit
- 3 × planting pots, at least 30–40cm (12–16in) in diameter
- Lightweight drainage material, e.g. clay aggregate
- Soil-based potting mix and slow-release fertilizer

PLANTS:

Large pot: *Eucalyptus gunnii*, *Heuchera villosa* "Palace Purple," *Viola* "Floral Power Super Lavender Blue"

Medium pot: Cyclamen, *Skimmia × confusa* "Kew Green"

Small pot: *Astelia chathamica*, *Aster* "Aqua Compact," *Helichrysum italicum*, *Heuchera* "Silver Veil"

TOP POT PLANTS FOR YEAR-ROUND INTEREST

- *Astelia chathamica*
- *Carex*, e.g. *C. testacea*, *C. oshimensis* "Evergold"
- *Cornus sanguinea* "Midwinter Fire"
- *Eucalyptus gunnii*
- *Heuchera* cvs, e.g. "Obsidian," "Chocolate Ruffles"
- *Myrtus communis*
- *Nandina domestica*
- *Pittosporum tenuifolium*
- *Sarcococca hookeriana* var. *humilis*
- *Skimmia × confusa* "Kew Green" (for flowers), *S. japonica* subsp. *reevesiana* (for red berries)
- *Stipa tenuissima*
- *Tiarella* "Mystic Mist"

TOP TIP

For an extra hit of spring color, poke crocus, daffodil, or tulip bulbs into the potting mix as you plant. As a general rule, bulbs are planted at a depth of three times their own height, with the pointy end upwards.

TIN CAN SALAD BAR

Cut costs and get creative with these fun, recycled tin can planters. Look out for them in delis, cafes, and foreign supermarkets, and get planting! Colorful and stylish, each grocery can holds an edible crop, from chilli peppers to salads and herbs.

The bright, colorful labels on these recycled grocery tin cans look great. Paper labels may fade and peel with time, so keep an eye out for cans with plastic labels, or better still metal-only cans, because these will last longer. Alternatively peel off the labels for a shiny, silver, contemporary look. Make sure you wash the cans well before planting, particularly any that previously held oil. Drill drainage holes in the base to help prevent plants from getting waterlogged. Adding a layer of drainage material, such as pea gravel, to the bottom of the can will also help.

Metal containers do get hot in summer, which can cause the potting mix to dry out quickly, so either place your salad bar out of direct sun or keep an eye on your crops through the summer months, watering them every day if necessary.

These containers won't last for ever, and the metal will eventually rust. Meanwhile they are perfect for sustaining an annual crop until it is harvested.

Right: **Keep an eye out** for colorful and unusual tin cans when you're shopping so you can create your own fun, edible windowsill garden.

PLANTING YOUR TIN CAN SALAD BAR

1 Stick masking tape on the base of each tin can. Then carefully drill drainage holes, through the tape and base, so that water will be able to drain freely.

2 Place a layer of pea gravel in the base of each can, to prevent the holes from getting clogged with potting mix. Add the potting mix, leaving enough room for your plants to be inserted at the same depth as they were in their previous pots.

3 Plant and firm in with extra potting mix. Water the plants well to help them settle.

TOP TIP

Tin cans can be used for seed sowing as well. Drill drainage holes in the base of each can and then overfill with seed or fine potting mix. Tap to settle the potting mix and firm it down with the base of an old pot. Water until the mix is moist and sow your seed sparingly onto the surface. Cover the seeds with a thin layer of potting mix and then cover with plastic wrap or a clear plastic bag sealed with a rubber band. Place your seed tin can in a warm, bright spot. Keep the potting mix moist until the seeds germinate.

A

SKINNY BALCONY PLANTERS

The right choice of pot is vital in a small space but it's not just how a container looks, it's how you use it. These tall, narrow planters are gorgeous but used together they will create instant drama.

A simple way to make a small space feel bigger is to divide it up into distinct areas, and a clever way to do this is with containers filled with seasonal or useful plants. These tall, skinny planters in an attractive faux stone are bold enough to make a great dividing wall or boundary when pushed together. Add some tall plants and instantly you have an effective, but attractive, screen that could be used to hide an unsightly wall or view. The bushy bamboo *Fargesia rufa* is a perfect screening plant, as it keeps its leaves right down to the base but is light enough not to dominate. Use two plants per pot or cut down on cost and split larger plants in half with a spade for a less immediate effect.

To create new intimate areas within a space, plant containers with eye-catching seasonal plants or else make the most of every inch of growing space by filling it with edible plants such as chilies, tomatoes, and herbs.

Above: **A planter for screening:** Use as many containers as you need, lined up together, to create an instant barrier or screen. Just leave a small gap between the planters to allow some light through.

Opposite: **Winter planter:** Brighten a dark corner on the dullest days with this cheery winter display. The clean, white flowers of the heather and cyclamen will lift the spirits while the stripy foliage of the sedge (*Carex*) softens the edges of the planter.

WHAT YOU WILL NEED

- 2 × tall, skinny, polystone planters
- Masking tape
- Drill and masonry bit
- Drainage material, e.g. old plastic plant pots
- Soil-based potting mix

PLANTS:

A White cyclamen, white heather (*Calluna vulgaris* "Alicia" Garden Girls Series), *Carex oshimensis* "Evergold"

B 2 × *Fargesia rufa* per pot

C Basil, chilli pepper, lettuce, mint, rosemary, thyme

continued overleaf ...

continued ...

Kitchen garden planter: These planters are filled with scented herbs, lettuce leaves, and chili peppers providing you with everything you might need for a summer of tasty pickings.

Other plants that you might like to try for a more rustic look include grape tomatoes, nasturtiums for their peppery tasting flowers, or crisp dwarf cucumbers.

PLANTING YOUR BAMBOO SKINNY BALCONY PLANTER

1 If your planter needs drainage holes, space strips of masking tape across the base to prevent the drill from slipping, then drill a series of holes in the base. Fill each planter with a generous layer of drainage material such as old plastic plant pots until about half full.

2 Top up each planter with potting mix, taking care to leave enough room for your plants. Soil-based potting mix is a good choice for bamboo because it holds water well and is heavier than multipurpose potting mix, minimizing the chance of these tall, thin planters toppling over in high winds.

3 Remove each bamboo plant from its pot and place in a planter at the correct depth, about 3cm (1¼in) from the rim. It may be necessary to trim the roots to make them fit the planter. Top up around the plants with potting mix, then water them in.

CRATES OF PRODUCE

You don't need a garden to grow your own food. These productive crates, crammed full of vegetables, herbs, and edible flowers, will keep you in fresh produce all summer long and are brilliantly easy to make and look after.

Wooden crates and boxes can be found new at garden centers as well as hardware and packaging shops, but it is worth looking for them in junkyards and antique shops too. Just make sure there is adequate depth for your crops — a minimum of 40cm (16in) is ideal for supporting most plants.

Before planting in any wooden container, always line it with plastic sheeting, to prevent the wood from rotting and to avoid having any chemicals in the wood leaching into the potting mix. Use a soil-based potting mix, and don't be tempted to overcrowd your crate — otherwise your crops will struggle.

Support chilies, beans, and eggplants with stakes if they need it, once fruit appears. Any fruit-bearing plants such as tomatoes and chili peppers will require a regular, high-potash feed as soon as the flowers appear. Keep picking the herbs and edible flowers to encourage more fresh leaves and blooms to develop.

PLANTING YOUR CRATES OF PRODUCE

1 Lay out the plastic sheeting and measure a liner for the base and the sides of each crate. Cut out according to shape.

2 Place the liner in one crate and use the staple gun to secure its sides and then its base to the crate. Trim the liner to fit. Cut and staple the liner for the other crate.

WHAT YOU WILL NEED

- Sheet of thick, black plastic
- Tape measure and pencil
- Wooden crates
- Scissors and staple gun
- Drainage material, e.g. styrofoam or old plastic plant pots
- Soil-based potting mix and slow-release fertilizer
- Stakes and twine (optional)

PLANTS:

Crate 1: Basil, chili pepper, cilantro, cornflower, rosemary

Crate 2: Eggplant, tomato, beans, chili pepper, lettuce leaves

3 Make a series of drainage holes in each liner with scissors.

continued overleaf ...

continued ...

4 Put a layer of styrofoam chips or other drainage material such as old plastic plant pots in the base of each crate.

TOP TIP

When choosing your crops, look for varieties that will grow well in pots: for example, go for grape or cherry tomatoes rather than larger types, which need a lot of space and attention.

OTHER GOOD CROPS FOR CRATES

Eggplant "Ophelia," carrot "Rondo," chilli pepper "Apache," zucchini "Patio Star," cucumber "Outdoor Star," runner bean "Hestia," sweet pepper "Mohawk" or "Redskin"

5 Add potting mix to each crate, filling to about two-thirds, to leave room for the vegetables and herbs to be planted. Then sprinkle on slow-release fertilizer and mix in.

6 Plant each crate — using stakes and twine to support plants such as beans and chilli peppers if they need it. Fill in with more potting mix, firm down, and water in.

Left: **Old wooden crates** lined with plastic to retain the soil and water make great planters. When filled with herbs, vegetables, and edible flowers, they become delightful mini-kitchen gardens.

WILDLIFE WINDOWBOX

The importance of gardens, however small, as habitats for wildlife is increasingly recognized, and with this project everyone can do their part. And it's not just the birds and the bees that benefit. You also get to enjoy the color and scent of flowers and foliage while you watch the wildlife come and go.

Our windowbox had both a nesting box and an insect hotel — a section filled with dead wood, bamboo canes, straw, and bits of stone and old tiles, which will provide crevices and nooks for insects to shelter and breed in.

The hole for the nesting box can be made with a circle bit or a wide drill bit. The hole should be 25–32mm (1–1¼in) in diameter, but its exact size will dictate the birds that use the nesting box: for example, a 25mm (1in) hole will attract house wrens and a 32mm (1¼in) hole will draw chickadees, tufted titmice and nuthatches.

A nesting box is most likely to be used if your window ledge is high up, rather than on the ground floor where people coming and going will discourage bird visits. Therefore, if your ledge is near ground level, omit the nesting box and extend your windowbox's planting areas or the size of the insect hotel.

During construction, line each planter with plastic to help preserve the wood, to prevent chemicals from leaching into the potting mix, and to keep moisture in the soil. A soil-based potting mix is heavier than a multipurpose one and will retain water and nutrients for longer as well as increasing stability. To ensure the windowbox is securely positioned, use small, galvanized, L-shaped brackets to attach it to the ledge.

WHAT YOU WILL NEED

- Tape measure and pencil
- Lengths of pressure-treated timber, 145 × 20mm (5¾ × ¾in)
- Wood saw
- Drill with circle bit or wide wood bits of 25mm (1in), 28mm (1¹⁄₁₀in), or 32mm (1¼in), and self-drilling screws
- Twigs, lengths of bamboo cane, stones, pieces of tile or terracotta pot
- Old plastic potting mix bag, for lining the planting spaces
- Scissors and pruning shears
- Staple gun
- Soil-based potting mix
- Topdressing, e.g. pea gravel
- Galvanized, L-shaped brackets

PLANTS: Insect-friendly ones, e.g. catnip, cornflower, geranium, Jacob's ladder, lavender, salvia, thyme, yarrow

KEY

Our wildlife windowbox was 84 × 18cm (34 × 7in) so we needed:

- 3 × 84cm (34in) lengths of pressure-treated timber, 145 × 20mm (5¾ × ¾in)
- 5 × 14cm (5½in) lengths of pressure-treated timber, 145 × 20mm (5¾ × ¾in); two of these pieces were for the ends while the other three were for internal supports
- 1 × 23cm (9in) length of pressure-treated timber, 145 × 20mm (5¾ × ¾in), for the nesting box roof

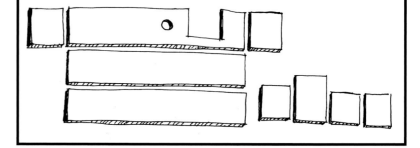

MAKING YOUR WILDLIFE WINDOWBOX

1 Calculate the size of your windowbox by measuring the window ledge. Mark and cut your pieces of wood to the appropriate sizes (see the key, left, for the timber sizes that we used for this project).

2 Attach the two end pieces to the base board for the windowbox, using the drill and self-drilling screws.

3 Use the pencil to mark on the base board where the three internal supports for the nesting box and insect hotel are to go. Screw these supports to the base.

4 On the front board, mark where the entrance hole for the nesting box and the opening for the insect hotel are to go. Use the drill to make a pilot hole for the nesting box entrance, then fit the wide drill bit and enlarge the hole. Cut out the hotel opening with a saw.

5 Screw the front board of the windowbox onto the base one and then screw on the back board.

6 Fill the insect hotel with the twigs and stones etc. Screw the roof of the nesting box in place.

continued overleaf ...

continued ...

7 Line each planting space with plastic, attaching it to the windowbox with the staple gun. Then cut holes in each liner for drainage.

8 Fill with potting mix and plant with your chosen insect-friendly plants. Topdress with pea gravel. Use the L-shaped brackets to fix the windowbox to the window ledge.

Above: **Hibernating insects** such as beetles and ladybugs will love the insect hotel in this windowbox and a bird may even take up residence in the neighboring nesting box, while bees, butterflies, and other pollinators will buzz happily among the flowers.

TOP TIP

The best plants to attract wildlife, particularly pollinating insects such as butterflies, bees, and hoverflies, are those that have flowers providing easy access to pollen. Avoid flowers that have double or multipetals. Don't worry about using only native plants — insects aren't fussy and will happily buzz around non-native plants as long as they are full of pollen and nectar.

CHUNKY TROUGH

No dirt? No problem. A long, low planter is the perfect alternative to a border on a balcony, roof, or in a yard. This chunky trough is simple to assemble and can be any size or shape — and it will expand your growing space considerably.

This trough is the solution anywhere that has no actual soil. Being squat, it mimics growing conditions in the ground, while its long, narrow length means you can use it to define edges and boundaries or to break up a space without the trough taking over. At this shape and size, the emphasis is on the plants it contains, particularly if you paint the trough to disappear into the background. However, the trough can be as tall or as wide as you like, and it can be used in any number of combinations.

Its easy-to-source, pressure-treated deck boards are lined with plastic to retain moisture, and to maximize the life of the trough by stopping the wood from rotting. As the contents of the trough are intended to last for a long time, it is filled with soil-based potting mix, which holds onto water and nutrients better than a soilless one. Place your trough in its chosen spot before planting.

Troughs can be planted with evergreens, grasses, a mix of perennials, or seasonal annuals. Ours included a mix of late summer perennials to bring a vibrant splash of color later in the year.

WHAT YOU WILL NEED

- Tape measure and pencil
- Pressure-treated deck boards, 19 × 120mm (¾ × 4¾in)
- Wood saw
- Lengths of post, 50 × 50mm (2 × 2in)
- Drill, wood bit, and deck screws
- Exterior wood stain or paint and brush
- Old plastic potting mix bag and scissors
- Staple gun
- Perlite (or vermiculite or other drainage material)
- Soil-based potting mix
- Horticultural pea gravel, for topdressing

PLANTS: *Achillea* "Paprika," *Cosmos bipinnatus* "Sonata White" (Sonata Series), *Dahlia* "Knockout," *D.* "Piccolo Pink," miscanthus, *Verbena bonariensis* "Lollipop"

Opposite: **When growing in the ground is limited** or impossible this easy-to-build planter is the answer and can bring a garden to even the most sterile space.

MAKING YOUR CHUNKY TROUGH

1 Measure the position where you want the trough to be placed. Then mark the decking boards for the trough into appropriate lengths.

2 Mark off and cut each piece with a saw. Then lay two (or more, depending on the height you want) of the front boards side by side and cut your posts to match their eventual height.

continued overleaf …

continued ...

3 Lay the two front boards side by side again over a post and use the drill to screw the boards to the post.

4 Do this at both ends of the boards. Stand the boards on their sides lengthways and screw in both the sides to each post. Make up the back and attach it to each post.

5 Turn the trough over and screw on the base boards but leave a slight gap between them to assist in drainage. Paint the trough with wood stain or paint.

6 Cut a plastic sheet from an old potting mix bag to fit the trough. Use the staple gun to attach it to the sides and then the base. With the scissors, make drainage slits in the plastic.

7 Put perlite in the base of the trough, to help with drainage. Fill the trough with a generous amount of potting mix.

8 Arrange your plants in the trough until you are happy with them, and then plant them. Topdress the potting mix with horticultural pea gravel to help hold moisture in the soil.

POND IN A POT

Water is an essential element in any garden, providing reflections, texture, and movement, but it's also a fantastic draw for birds and wildlife. This impressive container pond is easy to create, and it enables you to bring the beauty of water to even the smallest space.

This project will be tough to move once it's finished, so make it and plant it in position rather than having to shift it later. A sunny spot is good but don't site it in full sun because shade over some of the pond will help to reduce algae — a green, unsightly growth in the water.

Any large, shallow container can be used but if you have a porous clay pot — that is, one that has not been glazed — it will need sealing to prevent water being slowly lost through the sides. Bear in mind that metal containers hold the heat in summer so they are not suitable if you want to include fish in your pond.

If at all possible, use rainwater to fill your pond in a pot, because tap water is full of minerals that will encourage algae. If you have to resort to tap water, fill the pond very slowly with a hose and allow the water to stand for a week or two before adding the plants.

Plants will need repotting into aquatic baskets, which have lattice sides to allow water and air

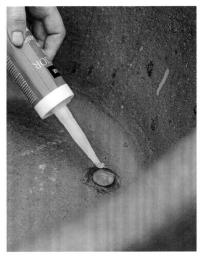

1 Plug any holes in the base of your pot with silicone sealant. Paint porous pots with sealant paint.

2 Place bricks or large rocks around the base of the pot where you want the marginal plants to go.

continued overleaf ...

WHAT YOU WILL NEED

- Large, shallow container (ours was 70cm/28in in diameter and 35cm/14in deep)
- Silicone sealant and, if necessary, sealant paint and paintbrush
- Bricks or large rocks
- Aquatic baskets
- Aquatic compost
- Gravel or pebbles, for topdressing

PLANTS:

Oxygenators: *Miriophyllum crispatum*

Marginal aquatic plants: *Alisma plantago-aquatica* var. *parviflorum, Cyperus papyrus, Equisetum scirpoides, Isolepis cernua*

Deep water plants: *Nymphaea tetragona* "Alba"

Floating aquatics: *Eichhornia crassipes, Salvinia natans*

movement. Instead of an ordinary multipurpose potting mix, use an aquatic mix that contains a slow-release fertilizer, which won't leach into the water. Topdressing with pebbles or gravel will help prevent the aquatic compost from floating away.

continued ...

TOP TIPS

- Although having such a pond will expand your plant repertoire brilliantly, you must choose the right plants for the depth of your pond. For example there are waterlilies suitable for depths of 10cm (4in) to more than 1m (3ft).
- Don't overplant your pond. You need only one floating plant every 1 × 1m (3 × 3ft) and at least two-thirds of the water surface should be kept clear to prevent algae
- Always purchase plants from a reputable aquatic nursery. Never buy overly vigorous or invasive plants.

3 Fill the pot with water. Collected rainwater is preferable, otherwise use tap water, feeding it in very slowly via a hose.

4 Half-fill each aquatic basket with aquatic mix. Remove all but the floating plants from their containers and plant into the baskets — more than one plant can go into the larger baskets.

5 Fill in with more aquatic mix, firm down, and topdress with gravel or pebbles.

6 Lower the baskets carefully onto the bricks in the base of the pond.

7 Drop the floating aquatics onto the surface of the water.

Opposite: **This simple pond in a pot** will help bring wildlife to your space as well as light and movement because it reflects the world around it.

DOWN ON THE GROUND

p.114

p.116

p.124

p.127

RAISED BED SEAT

A green lawn is still a favorite garden feature for many people, but it can be an impossible dream in a small space. This green seat brings the benefits of a lawn without the work, and offers somewhere soft to sit when you need a break.

There are numerous DIY raised bed kits available both online and in stores. Ours had a retro feel, and it could be either narrow in shape (as we made it) or square. There are also wooden kits, recycled plastic ones, and railroad tie sets, so choose whichever suits your space.

Sharp sand at the base of the structure will enhance drainage. Most of it can be filled with topsoil if you have it, to save money on potting mix. Make sure the surface of the soil is firm (so it doesn't sag later) and level (so that your seat is even). Firming with your heels or fists will help, while raking with a hand trowel will ensure you have an even finish.

Ideally sod is laid in autumn or spring when the soil is warm and moist; in summer the sod will need constant watering to prevent it from drying out before it has rooted in the soil.

When laying sod it's important to stagger the joins and to butt each piece of sod closely up against the next so there are no gaps. Once you have made your seat, leave the sod to settle for a couple of weeks before sitting on it.

Sod will obviously give an instant lawn but you could also sow a lawn from seed — it's a little more work but it will cost a fraction of the price.

PLANTING YOUR RAISED BED SEAT

1 Assemble your raised bed kit in position. Add a layer of sharp sand to the base, to help with drainage and increase stability.

2 Fill to the top of the raised bed with topsoil or potting mix. Firm down well, then rake with a hand trowel until the surface is level.

3 Lay the sod over the soil surface, taking care to butt pieces together tightly and to stagger joins.

Opposite: **You can** have a beautiful green lawn anywhere. This raised bed topped with turf doubles up as a seat while helping to break up an otherwise bare, gray spot.

WHAT YOU WILL NEED

- Raised bed kit and tools needed for its assembly
- Sharp sand
- Topsoil or potting mix
- Spade, hand trowel, and knife, for trimming the turf

PLANTS:

- Lawn sod or grass seed

TOP TIP

Cut the grass regularly with garden shears, to keep your lawn looking neat and tidy.

Scatter grass seed evenly across the soil, at the rate recommended on the seed packaging. The seed should take 7–10 days to germinate. Keep the soil well watered until the grass has become well established.

4 Trim the edges to fit the sides of the raised bed, using a knife for a clean, sharp finish.

GREEN ROOF

You won't waste an inch of space with this green roof project. If you devote the top of a garden or bike shed, or a log store, to plants, you will have a beautiful, green space that's good for you, the environment, and wildlife.

A planted roof is a fantastic way to add yet another green dimension to your garden, plus it will provide a habitat for insects and wildlife, improve air quality, and help cool the local environment. This project will work on whatever roof you've got — be it log store, shed, or even bird house. However the pitch of the roof should not be too steep — ideally no more than 20 degrees, to deter water run-off.

A planting frame is built around the roof to contain the plants. Its size must fit your individual roof, while its depth will depend on what you plan to plant. A DIY sedum roof kit, which is what we have used here, can be purchased from a specialist supplier and will not need soil, so a frame depth of 3–5cm (1¼–2in) is fine. Other plants, such as the heathers (*Calluna vulgaris*) and alpines that we've used (see pp118–9), require a reasonable soil depth — at least 10cm (4in) — if they are to thrive.

A sedum roof kit will come complete with a water-retention mat and a rolled mat of plants. It should be easy to work with, but if you have a large roof, you may need to enlist help when lifting and fitting the mat, to prevent it from splitting.

The alternative roofs of heather and alpines (see pp118–9) are planted as you would any shallow planter, placing potting mix on the plastic sheet and then planting one plant at a time as you work systematically across the roof.

Opposite: **A sedum mat** instantly greens an otherwise bare roof and provides a habitat for insects and invertebrates. In summer the plants will be in flower; in autumn the leaves take on reddish hues.

WHAT YOU WILL NEED

- Tape measure and pencil
- Lengths of pressure-treated wood, 19 × 100mm (¾ × 4in)
- Wood saw
- Drill, wood bit, and screws
- Black plastic sheeting
- Heavy-duty scissors

A **Sedum roof:** Water-retention mat, sedum mat

B **Heather roof:** Perlite or vermiculite, ericaceous compost, *Calluna vulgaris*

C **Alpine roof:** Multipurpose potting mix, perlite or vermiculite, alpine plants, e.g. echeveria, *sempervivum*, raoulia, saxifrage, sedum

MAKING YOUR GREEN ROOF FRAME

1 Measure your roof. Cut the wood to fit the roof edges.

2 Position each piece of wood against the relevant edge of the roof, ensuring that it is raised high enough to accommodate the depth of soil needed for the plants you intend to grow. Then screw it in place.

A

PLANTING YOUR SEDUM ROOF

3 Lay the black plastic sheeting over the roof and cut so that it fits within the frame — take it right up to the top of the frame edging, so it will contain all the potting mix and plants.

1 Cut the water-retention mat to fit the frame and place it over the plastic sheeting.

2 Carefully lay the sedum mat on the roof until it is sitting within the frame. Trim the mat to fit.

PLANTING YOUR HEATHER ROOF

1 Mix one part perlite or vermiculite with four parts ericaceous compost.

2 Starting at the lower edge, begin to plant the roof, adding the potting mix and plants one at a time. Fill in around each plant, and firm down.

3 Work up the roof, planting across it in rows until the area is covered.

TOP TIPS FOR GREEN ROOFS

- Always check that your roof is strong enough to support the weight of plants, soil, water etc. You may need to brace it with lengths of wood before you start.
- Don't screw the frame flush to the roof. A small 3mm (⅛in) gap between the frame and the roof will allow water to drain away freely.
- If you are planting a large roof, fix battens across it to hold the plastic lining in place.
- For a natural look, add potting mix and then leave it to nature to colonize — with seeds blown in by the wind or dropped by visiting wildlife.

PLANTING YOUR ALPINE ROOF

Follow steps 1–3 of Planting your heather roof (see opposite) but use multipurpose potting mix combined with pea gravel. Then topdress between the plants with more pea gravel, to keep moisture away from the plants.

Opposite: **The upright spikes of this heather** (*Calluna vulgaris*) bring texture and floral interest to this green roof. Cut back the flowered shoots in spring to keep the plants in shape.

Right: **Alpines and succulents,** happy in the wild in the cracks between rocks and in dry, shallow ground, will thrive on this shed roof. Simply divide clumps every two to three years to boost the display.

PAVING-SLAB GARDEN

Bring green to the gray with this imaginative solution to softening and brightening an otherwise hard, bare space. Simply lift the odd slab or brick and allow plants to run free.

This project can be adopted anywhere that has a surface of laid stone, slab, or brick. The idea is to remove either one or a number of such pavers and put plants in their place. This can be done in gardens and backyards where there is otherwise no planting. It can also be used in conjunction with beds and borders, to continue the planting and introduce additional green spaces.

Lift single slabs or bricks or, if you have room, remove a series of adjacent ones to leave an L-shaped, herringbone-shaped, or randomly shaped spot in which to plant.

Any paver laid on sand and jointed with mortar should be easy to raise by wedging the tip of a spade beneath a slab edge or at a corner and prying it up. If the paving is impossible to lift, jimmy out the cement between the slabs, and plant in the resulting spaces.

The earth beneath any paving will be poor and dry, so rake over the area thoroughly and add a generous amount of well-rotted organic matter such as garden compost, animal manure, or leafmold — anything that will feed the soil and help to improve its structure.

Your choice of plants will depend on the aspect and size of each new planting area. For very small spaces, choose plants that are tough enough to withstand foot traffic. Look for plants such as thyme and mint, which release volatile, scented oils whenever their leaves are crushed.

You may need to split plants to squeeze them into your planting site, but most groundcover plants, which spread naturally, will divide readily. Just pull or snip each rootball apart, making sure that each piece has both a bit of stem and a bit of root. Otherwise sow annual seeds in the cracks and keep well watered initially.

WHAT YOU WILL NEED

- Spade or trowel — whatever tool you use to lift up a slab
- Garden fork
- Well-rotted garden compost or other organic matter

PLANTS:

Tough, scented plants, e.g. *Chamaemelum nobile* "Treneague," creeping thyme (*Thymus* "Bressingham," *T.* "Doone Valley"), *Mentha pulegium*, *M. requienii*, *Soleirolia soleirolii*

Groundcover plants, e.g. *Campanula portenschlagiana*, *C. poscharskyana*, lady's mantle, Mexican fleabane, *Pachysandra terminalis*

Contemporary, drought-tolerant plants, e.g. echeveria, *sempervivum*, rosularia, *Sedum acre*

Evergreen shrubs, e.g. *Nandina domestica*, osmanthus, pittosporum, *Viburnum tinus*

Annuals (from seed), e.g. *Briza maxima*, California poppy, *Cerinthe major* "Purpurescens," *Cosmos bipinnatus* "Dazzler," love-in-a-mist, *Orlaya grandiflora*

Opposite, top left: **Leaving gaps** in between slabs and filling in with gravel and creeping plants such as thyme will green up the gray and allow water to flow through.

Opposite, top right: **This paved space** has been broken up by removing a series of slabs and planting low-growing and evergreen plants throughout.

Opposite, bottom left: **A "rill"** of tough alpines and succulents flows through the hard landscaping, creating a clever seam of color.

Opposite, bottom right: **The ground beneath** lifted slabs has been planted with a mix of herbs, making great use of space in a small area.

HERBY TABLE PLANTER

Pluck fresh, tasty leaves while you eat at this quirky patio table. When beautifully planted with herbs, cut-and-come-again lettuce leaves, or edible flowers, a sunken trough such as this herby table planter makes a stylish, living, edible centerpiece.

This project can easily be adapted to any table, whether plastic or wood. We chose a slatted timber one, but slats can be tricky to cut. A solid wooden table would be easier while a plastic table is even simpler, but the latter will be light and so more susceptible to blowing over.

We set the planter in the center of the table but it could be placed to one side or at an end. Although we used a single zinc windowbox, a row of circular terracotta pots would also look great — use a suitably sized and shaped drill bit to make the holes. To ensure the hole is the correct size, measure just below the rim of your planter — those with a lip work well because the lip rests on the table and doesn't need any extra support.

Remember to drill drainage holes in your planter if it does not already have them. Use potting mix appropriate to the plants you choose.

Right: **Fragrant herbs** are the centerpiece of this wooden table, but a clever sunken planter could also be filled with colorful flowers — even strawberries.

WHAT YOU WILL NEED

- Recycled patio table (ours was a slatted wooden one)
- Tape measure and pencil
- Planter with a lip, e.g. a zinc windowbox
- Jigsaw
- Drill, masonry bit, and screws
- Soil-based or multipurpose potting mix, depending on choice of plants
- Wooden batten (optional) — see Top Tip opposite

PLANTS:

Herbs, e.g. oregano, parsley, rosemary, sage, thyme

Edible flowers, e.g. cornflower, lavender, pansy, pot marigold

MAKING YOUR HERBY TABLE PLANTER

1 Turn your table upside down. Use a tape measure to work out where its center is — measure the width and the length and halve them to find the middle. It may be easier to measure the center diagonally, depending on the shape and type of your table. Mark the spot.

2 Measure the size of your planter just below its lip, to establish the size of the hole you need.

3 Center the planter over the mark on the table, and draw around it.

4 Turn the table onto its side and cut out the marked hole for the planter, with a jigsaw.

5 Drill drainage holes in the base of the planter. To help keep the drill bit steady, you could add a piece of masking tape over the area to be drilled.

6 Turn the table upright. Insert the planter in the central hole, fill with soil-based or multipurpose potting mix, and plant.

TOP TIP

If the table is slatted, provide extra support around the planter by cutting and screwing in battens around the hole.

GABION COFFEE TABLE

Although smothered in plants, this gabion cube has a practical twist — it doubles as a stunning coffee table or seat, and is perfect for use on a balcony or in a small yard.

Planted gabion baskets have been on display at flower shows and pictured in magazines for a while, but this inspired take on the theme is filled with plants and then topped with a paving tile, so it is transformed into a gorgeous, "green" coffee table.

Choose plants that trail (e.g. the nepeta), spread (e.g. the ajuga), or have dense foliage (e.g. the heuchera) so that they quickly cover the cube with their greenery.

Gabion baskets of various shapes and sizes are available from builders' merchants as well as online, and they are easy to put together. We lined our cube with landscape fabric (to contain the potting mix) as well as with a square of plastic in the base (to help hold in moisture). We then gradually filled it with a free-draining potting mix (of four parts potting mix to one part pea gravel), rather than with the traditional stones, and inserted the plants through slits or crosses made in the fabric. The plants were pushed in from the outside and then covered with the potting mix and firmed down, before the next layer was planted.

When the cube is fully planted it is topped with a tile or whatever suits your surroundings and purpose. Try chunky timber for a comfortable seat or a tile or paving slab to match your terrace. Just be sure to secure it to the top with "table clamps" that can be attached through the gabion cube and to the stone.

The cube can be watered from the outside, or else remove the top and give the plants a good water from above.

MAKING YOUR GABION COFFEE TABLE

1 Following the manufacturer's instructions, assemble your gabion cube, including threading the screw wires through each corner.

Opposite: **This gabion cube**, being densely filled with compact-growing evergreen plants, is a lush mix of leaf colors, shapes, and textures year-round.

continued overleaf …

continued ...

2 Line the cube with landscape fabric, folding it over the top and roughly cutting it to size. Then place a square of black plastic sheeting in the base of the cube.

3 Pour the first layer of potting mix into the base of the cube and work in slow-release fertilizer.

4 From the outside, plant the first layer of the cube, cutting a small slit or cross in the landscape fabric for each plant.

5 Carefully push a plant through each slit. Fill in around the rootball with the potting mix/fertilizer combination, then firm down. Continue planting. Once a layer is complete, fill the cube with more potting mix/fertilizer combination.

6 Continue planting the cube until you reach the top. Trim off the fabric at the top. Then position a tile or slab over the top of your gabion cube and secure with the table clamps.

TOP TIP

If you are using large or delicate plants and are worried about damaging their rootballs, protect the roots before you plant. As you fill your gabion cube, carefully wrap the roots of each plant in a strip of newspaper or some paper towel before inserting it through the wire and slit in the landscape fabric. Once the plant is positioned, remove the paper and fill in around the rootball with the potting mix/fertilizer combination, firming as you go.

BALCONY BENCH

Perfect for a balcony or small roof terrace, this clever bench is both a planter and a seat. With evergreen ferns for year-round color and tall bamboos to provide privacy, it is the ideal place to rest at the end of the day.

This simple bench is essentially just a box — a wooden rectangular frame clad with wooden slats, with a planter at one end that has been made by dividing the bench up and creating another box inside. This is also clad on the outside, to ensure that it is completely contained, and then lined with plastic to protect the wood.

   Both the bench and the planter can be of any size. Just make sure it is a comfortable height to sit on — about 45cm (18in) high is a good height for most of us (as well as the perfect depth for plants such as our bamboo). Also don't overdo the size of the planter in relation to the seating area or you will be in danger of feeling swamped! Fill the planter with a mix of four parts potting mix to one part perlite (or pea gravel).

   Plant with shade-loving evergreens, as we have done, or try some sun-loving plants if your balcony is in a bright spot. Add cushions or matting for extra comfort to the back and/or seat.

WHAT YOU WILL NEED

- Tape measure and pencil
- Lengths of pressure-treated wood, 50 × 75mm (2 × 3in)
- Wood saw
- Drill, wood bit, and screws
- Wood slats, 19 × 38mm (¾ × 1½in), for the bench cladding
- Black plastic sheeting
- Staple gun
- Scissors
- Multipurpose potting mix combined with drainage material, e.g. perlite or horticultural pea gravel, in a ratio of 4:1

PLANTS FOR SHADE:

Ferns, e.g. *Athyrium*, *Dryopteris*

Bamboos, e.g. *Fargesia*, *Shibataea*; *Aucuba japonica* "Rozannie"; *Fatsia japonica*; *Viburnum tinus* "Eve Price"; *Buxus sempervirens*; *Sarcococca confusa*

PLANTS FOR SUN:

Bamboos, e.g. *Phyllostachys aurea*, *Fargesia rufa*

Grasses, e.g. *Carex testacea*, *Deschampsia cespitosa*, *Anemanthele lessoniana*; *Phormium tenax*; *Lavender angustifolia*

MAKING YOUR BALCONY BENCH

1 Measure your space to establish the size of the bench.

2 Measure and cut out the board lengths for the top and base frames of the bench. Screw them together to make two rectangles.

continued overleaf...

continued ...

3 Cut vertical supports to the desired height of your bench. Screw them to the frames, joining them together to make a box shape

4 Put another set of supporting boards two-thirds of the way along the frame to box off the planter within the bench. Then screw slats around the sides and along the top of the bench as well as inside to define the planter.

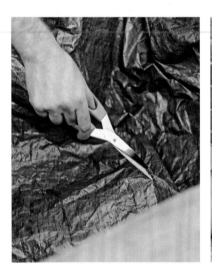

5 Line the inside of the planter with black plastic sheeting and secure with the staple gun. Make holes with scissors, for drainage. Finish the planter off neatly by screwing slats around its edge.

6 Move your bench into position. Fill the planter with the potting mix, then plant.

Right: **Stylish as well as chic**, this nifty slatted bench is both a seat and planter and can be made to fit any space no matter how small.

BELOW BENCH PLANTER

Although often considered dead space, the ground beneath your garden seat no longer needs to be bare. With careful plant choices and a little extra nutrition, such a dry, shady spot can become a thriving jungle of green.

The soil in these sites is notoriously poor and dry — similar to that at the foot of a wall or beneath a tree — it therefore needs to be improved before planting to give plants the best possible start. Having turned over the ground, you should incorporate plenty of organic matter. This will slowly release much-needed nutrients as well as helping to improve the soil structure, which then retains water and nutrients for longer.

After planting, mulch the plants to stop moisture from evaporating from the soil and to give plants an extra boost. For the first year at least, continue to water and mulch the plants in dry spells so that they establish well.

When choosing plants remember that the other problem they face is a lack of light so always look for plants that can cope with being in shade for at least part of the day. It's worth watching as the sun moves around your garden seat to see exactly how much sun the plants underneath get.

WHAT YOU WILL NEED

- Hand trowel or garden spade
- Well-rotted organic matter, e.g. garden compost, horse manure, or leafmold

PLANTS:

Dry shade lovers, e.g. bergenia, *Brunnera macrophylla* "Jack Frost," *Epimedium × rubrum*, *Galium odoratum*, *Hakonechloa macra*, heuchera, *Lamium maculatum*, *Pachysandra terminalis*, *Viburnum tinus*, *Vinca major*, *V. minor*

Ferns, e.g. *Asplenium scolopendrium*, *Athyrium filix-femina*, *Dryopteris erythrosora*, *Polypodium vulgare*, *Polystichum setiferum*

PLANTING YOUR BELOW BENCH PLANTER

1 Cultivate the soil beneath the bench with a hand trowel or garden spade. Then dig in plenty of well-rotted organic matter.

2 Remove each plant from its pot and plant it, firming the soil around the rootball as you go.

3 Water the plants in well, then mulch with more organic matter. Continue to water regularly to help the plants establish.

Opposite: **Ferns, dead nettle (*Lamium*), and *Brunnera macrophylla* "Jack Frost"** bring instant life to the tricky space beneath this bench.

MOBILE GARDEN

Rustic containers with a hidden extra, these mobile planters have wheels so that they can be moved around — to change the shape of your space, create intimacy, or transfer plants in and out of the sun.

Although you could make just one of these movable planters, for the greatest effect you need at least two. We built one square planter and one long rectangular one. These can be used together in any number of combinations. They can be positioned so they divide an area or change its atmosphere by bringing them in close or else by moving them out to the edges to open things up.

If you want to grow large established plants, such as the olive we used, make sure you measure the size of its rootball at an early planning stage and also factor in space for it to develop, before you make the planter.

Leave a slight gap between each base planter board, for drainage. Also line the planter with plastic and cut holes in it, to enhance water flow.

These mobile garden planters are intended for permanent planting schemes, so are filled with soil-based potting mix. We planted them with a mix of perennials, grasses, and succulents, as well as a gorgeous established olive tree, but they could contain whatever plants you love best — appropriate to the growing conditions.

WHAT YOU WILL NEED

- Tape measure and pencil
- Lengths of pressure-treated board, 50 × 75mm (2 × 3in)
- Wood saw
- Drill, wood bit, and screws
- Lengths of reclaimed floorboards
- Wheels and screws
- Black plastic sheeting, staple gun, and scissors
- Drainage material, e.g. old, plastic plant pots
- Soil-based potting mix

PLANTS: *Aeonium* "Zwartkop," *Crocosmia* "Lucifer," *Cosmos atrosanguineus*, lavender, *miscanthus*, olive tree, red hot poker, *Stipa tenuissima*

MAKING YOUR MOBILE GARDEN

1 Having established the size of the planter you want to build, measure and cut out the board lengths for its top and base frame.

5 Use lengths of floorboard to make a neat trim around the top of the planter. Then screw each in position.

6 Turn the planter upside down and attach a wheel to each corner, with screws.

2 Screw the pieces together to make two rectangles or squares, as appropriate. Cut the vertical supports to the length you need and then screw them to the top and base frames, joining everything together to form the planter frame.

3 Measure and cut out lengths of floorboard. Place them on the base frame and screw them in position, leaving gaps between each floorboard, for drainage.

4 Continue to cut and screw in the floorboards all around the sides of the planter frame.

7 Line the planter with plastic sheeting, and secure with a staple gun. Cut holes through this liner for drainage.

8 Add a layer of drainage material to the base of the planter. Fill with potting mix, and then plant.

TOP TIPS

- Because you can't see the base of the planter, use marine plywood to save money — it could well be a fraction of the cost of even recycled lumber.
- You could also substitute new tongue-and-groove boards, and paint it to match your color scheme.

Overleaf left: **Mobile planters** allow you to create a changing scene in your garden. Simply wheel them into position as and when required.

Overleaf right: **The jubilant combination** of red hot poker (*Kniphofia*), feathery *Stipa tenuissima*, and chocolate cosmos (*Cosmos atrosanguineus*) brings color, movement, and sound.

WHAT DO YOU NEED?

ESSENTIAL KIT
- **Watering can** — or better still an outdoor faucet and hose
- **Hand tools**: trowel and fork
- **Pruning shears**
- **Plant supports**: stakes, canes, twigs, trellis, wire, and eye screws
- **Garden twine**
- **Plant fertilizer**: a general, high-nitrogen feed and a high-potash liquid feed for flowers and fruit
- **Broom**, or dustpan and brush, for sweeping up leaves and spilt soil
- **Bucket** or tub for carrying tools and when mixing compost

The tools that you need to get growing depend on what you're going to grow, but whatever you are planning it's worth investing in some helpful tools before you start.

Hand trowel and fork are required for planting, digging, and weeding in pots and raised beds; for bigger borders, a garden fork and spade will make work easier and you will not need to bend down all the time. Pruning shears, viewed by many gardeners as their single most important tool, are essential for pruning and tidying plants. Choose a pair that's comfortable to hold and has high-quality steel blades. Many people prefer the scissor action, bypass type, as opposed to the crushing action of anvil pruning shears, but see which works best for you. None of these tools needs to be bought new, so keep an eye out for them in thrift shops and second-hand stores. If you sharpen and oil them regularly, they should last for years.

A watering can with a rose on the end of the spout is ideal if you are looking after a few pots. For anything more, it's worth installing an outdoor faucet and hose, and if you're away a lot or very busy, why not invest in a drip or automatic irrigation system (see p159)?

If you're growing climbers, tall plants, or plants that produce heavy fruit or large flowers, they'll need support. Canes or other stakes and twine will stop plants from toppling over, but to encourage climbers to blanket an area, erect trellis or wires on which they can wind around.

Finally, all plants, especially those grown in containers and have limited resources, will benefit from a little extra help. Your own home-made garden compost and local green waste are good for improving the soil, whereas well-rotted animal manure or mushroom compost are great for feeding plants, as well as improving the structure and moisture-holding capacity of the soil. Organic fertilizers such as bonemeal, blood fish and bone, or seaweed will release nutrients slowly throughout the growing season. Regular applications of a high-potash fertilizer such as a liquid tomato food will help promote better flowering (see p160 for further tips on feeding plants).

Left: **All you need** to get started are a few essential tools: pruning shears, twine to help plants climb and get support, and labels to help you to keep track of what you're growing.

Left: **Pots are a helpful solution** when space in the ground is limited. When grouped together they can create the same jungle-like effect as plants growing in a bed or border.

TYPES OF DRAINAGE MATERIAL

Crocks

These broken shards of terracotta pot are the traditional choice for many gardeners. Just hold on to old, cracked pots and break them up when you need them.

Gravel

A good alternative drainage material if you don't have crocks. It can become heavy in large containers so is best for small ones.

Stones or brick

These are easy to source and are a good way to increase stability in your container when growing top-heavy plants or positioning pots in a windy spot.

Styrofoam chunks

Recycle parcel packaging or styrofoam plant trays by breaking them up and using them as a lightweight drainage material, which is perfect in large pots or where weight is an issue on balconies and roofs.

Old plastic pots

Many gardeners have an excess of these and using them as drainage material is a great way to recycle them. They are also light and bulky so ideal in large containers.

POTS

When space is severely lacking, pots and other containers literally become the garden, but they are also an essential feature in any small space. They are versatile, flexible, easy to look after, and can be planted to green and animate a space instantly.

Almost anything will grow in a pot, provided it is chosen with care in the first place. Style is important, but first and foremost a container must be the right size and material for the plants you plan to grow in it.

Always choose a pot large enough for your plants, and remember that the smaller the pot, the higher the demand for water and nutrients will be — and the more work for you.

Consider a container's weight if you plan to move it around, have to carry it upstairs, or if it is to be placed on a balcony or roof patio.

POT DRAINAGE

Whatever the container's shape, size, or material, make sure it has drainage holes in the bottom, because good drainage is absolutely vital in pots. Drill holes yourself if necessary.

Water must be able to drain away freely, so line the base of every container with a layer of drainage material to prevent the holes in the bottom from getting blocked with compost or plant roots (see box right for suggested drainage materials).

If your pots are to be positioned in a damp, shady spot, use pot feet to raise them up and create a gap between the pot and the ground, so that water can drain away.

If you place pot saucers under containers to catch water in summer, remember to remove them in autumn so they don't hold excess water and leave plants sitting in freezing wet soil.

POT MATERIALS

When you're growing in a small space aesthetics matter. You're going to be looking at your containers every day, particularly those in the prime positions closest to your doors and windows. Pots come in a whole range of materials and each has its own look and style, advantages and drawbacks.

Terracotta: A traditional choice, terracotta, or clay, pots are elegant and timeless. In addition, they are heavy and stable, so suitable for large, tall plants but not so handy if you need to carry or move a pot about. Terracotta

Below left: **Metal containers** such as this one complement plants perfectly and go well with silver-leaved plants and purple sweet potato vine (*Ipomoea batatas*).

Below center: **This old wooden crate** has been lined with plastic, to prolong its life, and then beautifully planted with a mix of grasses, perennials, and low-growing sedums for a rustic look.

Below right: **Anything, even this old bread bin**, can be recycled and turned into a unique quirky container for the garden.

is naturally porous so it is good for drainage, allowing air to get to a plant's roots. (Glazed terracotta is less porous.) However terracotta also draws water away from the soil and in hot, dry weather can leave plants parched. Look for frostproof rather than frost-resistant pots — they are not the same — otherwise pots can crumble in cold winters.

Metal: This material brings a contemporary or vintage feel to your planting, depending on the pot's styling, and includes stainless steel (shiny, painted, or rusted), cast iron, lead, and copper. All are tough and retain water well. However metal gets cold in winter and heats up in the sun, which can dry out soil, so insulate and line pots with bubble wrap, cardboard, or newspaper. Metal containers can also be heavy.

Wood: This often adds a rustic touch. Hardwood such as oak or teak is less prone to rotting than softwood, due to its high oil and rubber content.

The cheaper but less tough, pressure-treated softwood requires treatment and maintenance over time. Hardwood is heavier and generally more expensive than softwood. Both wood types should be protected with a plastic liner to prevent the wood rotting and any chemicals from leaching into the soil.

Plastic & fiberglass: Being cheap, tough, long-lasting, and light, these pots are perfect for a balcony, roof terrace, or any place where weight is an issue. Both plastic and fiberglass retain water well but can be prone to waterlogging, so ensure there are plenty of drainage holes in each pot. Glass-reinforced plastic (GRP) or polymer is a great choice for contemporary-style roof terraces and balconies because it can be made in any shape, helping to maximize space.

Stone looks beautiful, ages gracefully, retains water, and insulates plants well, but it can be very expensive and heavy. Look out for slate and reconstituted stone, which is cheaper.

Right: **When well planted**, pots of different sizes, colors, and materials can be displayed together to very pleasing effect.

OTHER CONTAINER CHOICES

Hanging baskets: These are great for making optimum use of your space but they must have a coir, sisal, or plastic liner. (It is fine to line your baskets with the more traditional sphagnum moss, but please do ensure it is from a sustainable source.) Hanging baskets do not hold water well so require extra attention.

Pocket planters: Relatively new on the gardening scene, these hanging planters, composed of small, square pockets, are ideal for greening walls, fences, and railings and are the easiest way to start vertical gardening (see p64). They are available in a range of materials, from canvas and oilcloth to felt, and in a host of colors. They do not hold much soil so are best for low-maintenance and drought-resistant plants.

Recycled containers: Plants can be grown in just about anything, from old baths and sinks to boxes, buckets, baskets, tins, and crates. Recycling or "upcycling" containers is a great way to get creative and stamp your personality on your growing space. Although such containers may not last as long as some new ones, they are generally cheaper, if not free, and have an individual look that is truly priceless. Just make sure that the recycled containers are big enough and have adequate drainage holes for your plants. Always put style first and exercise constraint — plants may well

grow happily in old boots or stacked-up tires but that doesn't mean that they should!

- Wash each recycled container carefully with warm, soapy water before planting. A wire brush is helpful for particularly dirty spots and for scrubbing away any flaky rust in old metal ones. If a vessel is fragile, a rust-killer is less brutal but make sure the inside of the pot is washed again afterwards.
- Ensure your recycled pots are safe by filing down any sharp edges and corners and by removing any old nails or tacks. If you think your pot may have contained something toxic, such as oil or acid, then wash

it really well and avoid growing edibles in it.
- Drainage holes are essential so use a drill and an appropriate bit or a hammer and heavy-duty nail to make a series of holes in the base of each container, spacing them an inch or so apart.
- If you want to paint your recycled pot, anything other than terracotta is best rubbed down with sandpaper first and then wiped with mineral spirits, to help the surface absorb the paint.
- If a container is made of wood or wicker, line it with plastic, stapled to the sides, to prevent rot. Lining metal pots will help to regulate the soil temperature.

CHOOSING & BUYING PLANTS

WHERE TO SOURCE

Plant buying options are increasingly varied — you can shop online and by mail order or at the more traditional garden centers and specialty nurseries. Plants including bulbs are also available at supermarkets and homeware shops as well as flea markets, summer fairs, garden shows, and local plant fairs run by fellow gardeners. If you're lucky, you may even spot plants for sale in front gardens and by the side of the road.

At the garden center, plants are available year-round, although such retail outlets tend to stock plants when they are at their peak and in flower and less at their dormant times of year. You can see the plants and check their condition before you buy, but choice is limited to what they have in stock.

Mail order, either online or from plant catalogs, is an easy, relaxed way to acquire plants and gives you access to all the top nurseries and specialty growers from the comfort of your armchair. However, you can't see the plants yourself and have to rely on trusting the seller, so always buy from companies with a good reputation. Mail-order season tends to be between mid-autumn and early spring, but some companies may offer container stock year-round.

Specialty nurseries often sell one type or range of plants: for example, grasses, or plants for shade. They are run by enthusiasts, who are very knowledgeable and tend to stock plants that may be difficult to find elsewhere. Such nurseries are therefore good places to go if you need advice or are looking for something very particular.

PLUG PLANTS

If you are looking for seasonal bedding or vegetable plants, keep an eye out for plug plants. Usually ready to buy from spring onwards, they are mini, sometimes tiny, young plants that are bought to grow on at home. They come in a range of sizes depending on how advanced their growth is and how much care they need — larger plugs can often be planted straight into their basket or pot, while mini plugs, available in early spring, will need growing on for a few weeks first. If you have the space and the time, they are a great way to get cheap plants, without having to start from scratch with seed.

BUYING TIPS

Remember that many types of plants have a specific season of sale: for example, bare-root plants are available only between mid-autumn and early spring, and spring-flowering bulbs from early autumn. Container-grown plants are available year-round but try to avoid buying plants in the heat of summer.

- Look for plants that are in the very best condition, with full, even growth and healthy, lush foliage.
- Avoid plants with pale green, yellow, or wilting leaves or showing any signs of pests or diseases (e.g. holey or raggedy leaves).
- A thick layer of moss and liverwort on the surface of the soil is a sign the plant has been in the pot for a long time and may be pot bound.
- Pick up a plant and feel its weight — if it's very light, it hasn't been watered for a while, and if it slides easily out of its pot, it's parched.
- Look for roots coming out of the pot base. A thick knot of congested roots means the plant is root bound and growth may be stunted.
- Knock a plant out of its pot to check for the telltale white grubs of vine weevil larvae.
- Don't be seduced by flowers. Plants

already in bloom won't establish so well, and you'll get a better flower display that will last longer if you buy plants that are not yet in bud.

- Don't be afraid to buy small. Big is not always better when shopping for plants. Plugs and smaller plants will often establish quickly and well.
- Always unpack plants that have come by mail right away, and revive them with water. Plant them as soon as possible.

Top: **Young, small plants** are often a good choice, because they establish readily and quickly grow into strong, thriving plants.

Above left: **Always acquire the best** plants you can, checking them for any signs of wilt, pale foliage, or pest and disease attack before you buy them.

Above right: **Bare-root plants** are much cheaper than plants grown in pots, but are available only at certain times of the year. These strawberry runners are on sale from late summer until spring.

CONTAINER VERSUS BARE-ROOT PLANTS

If you're shopping for plants in the dormant season — that is, between mid-autumn and early spring — you will often see two types of plants for sale: those in containers and bare-root ones.

Plants in containers

Containerized plants and container-grown plants are not the same. Container grown means exactly that — the plant or tree has been grown in the pot you buy it in. Containerized plants have usually been lifted from the ground and then planted into a pot with soil around their roots. These are usually cheaper than container-grown plants but are generally available only in autumn and winter. Plants in containers don't need to be planted as urgently as bare-root plants.

Bare-root plants

These plants have been lifted from the ground and come wrapped in cloth with no soil around their roots. They are available only between mid-autumn and early spring. There is always a much wider choice of varieties available than for containerized plants, and they are considerably cheaper. However bare-root plants must be planted as soon as they reach your home.

PLANTS FOR A PURPOSE

The key when choosing plants is always to grow the right plant in the right place. Picking plants purely because you like them is all too tempting but doomed to failure in the long run. Forcing a plant to grow somewhere it dislikes will result in frustration, lots of work, and a weak, struggling plant at best.

Get to know your space by assessing and taking stock of the conditions. Note the areas of shade, where the soil is damp or dry, and the route of the sun as it passes across your space. Finally, think about what you want your planting to achieve and select your plants accordingly.

SHADE

Every garden has some areas of shade, and small gardens often even more so. Watch where the light and shade fall on your site, so that you know exactly what your conditions are and where. The difference between light and dense shade can be immense (see box on p13) so opt for appropriate plants (see box right).

TOP PLANTS FOR SHADE

- *Akebia quinata*
- *Anemone hupehensis* var. *japonica, A.* × *hybrida*
- *Brunnera macrophylla* cvs, e.g. "Jack Frost," "Looking Glass"
- *Carex oshimensis* "Evergold"
- *Cercidiphyllum japonicum*
- *Dryopteris erythrosora, D. wallichiana*
- *Epimedium* × *rubrum*
- × *Fatshedera lizei*
- *Geranium phaeum*
- *Helleborus orientalis*
- *Heuchera* cv, e.g. "Plum Pudding"
- *Hosta* "Halcyon" (Tardiana Group)
- *Liriope muscari*
- *Parthenocissus* spp.
- *Viburnum tinus*

Far left: **Lilyturf** (*Liriope muscari*) thrives in shade and is ideal in a pot or as the edging at the front of a dark border.

Left: **Heucheras** are a great choice for shady sites, bringing year-round color – spikes of pretty flowers in summer, and a dazzling choice of leaf color.

WIND

Whether you're growing on a balcony, up on a rooftop, or simply want to plant a windowbox, your main challenge will be the wind (see p12). Plants that grow in such exposed situations have to be tough and tenacious. Many of these determined plants have the typical adaptations of drought-tolerant ones (see p147). Others however, are low growing and cling to the ground, while some produce bending stems (that flex in the wind) or large, sail-like leaves.

Providing shelter in the form of screens and hedging will expand the range of plants you can grow beyond those mentioned in the box (see right).

Below left: **The blue spheres** of globe thistle (*Echinops banaticus*) cope well in the windy, exposed conditions on balconies and rooftops.

Below center: **Hawthorn** (*Crataegus*) is a tough tree with a dense, thorny habit, pretty flowers, and attractive fruit, or haws. It is perfect where space is an issue.

Below right: **Sea holly** (*Eryngium*) is a beautiful plant for a blustery spot. It dies back gracefully to leave ghostly seedheads that will remain throughout winter.

TOP PLANTS FOR EXPOSED SITES

Shelterbelt plants
Crataegus spp
Pinus mugo, P. sylvestris
Salix caprea
Thuja plicata

Trees
Arbutus unedo
Betula pendula
Quercus ilex
Sorbus aucuparia

Shrubs
Euonymus japonicus
Griselinia littoralis
Hippophae rhamnoides
Lavandula spp.
Pittosporum tobira "Nanum"
Pyracantha spp.
Sambucus nigra
Tamarix tetrandra

Grasses
Cortaderia selloana
Elymus hispidus
Miscanthus sinensis
Stipa tenuissima

Perennials
Anemone hupehensis var. *japonica,*
　A. × *hybrida*
Crocosmia spp.
Echinops ritro
Eryngium maritimum
Erysimum "Bowles's Mauve"
Euphorbia spp.
Kniphofia spp.
Libertia spp.
Phormium tenax
Rudbeckia spp.
Sedum "Matrona"
Verbena bonariensis

Windowbox plants
Agapanthus africanus
Alchemilla mollis
Antirrhinum majus
Armeria maritima
Chionodoxa forbesii
Cosmos atrosanguineus
Crocus spp.
Gazania spp.
Ophiopogon planiscapus
　"Nigrescens"
Phlox paniculata

DROUGHT TOLERANCE

Any spot that is in the shadow of a tree or at the base of a wall will be blighted with dry soil, while sites that are exposed, up high, and regularly beaten by the wind will also suffer. These situations require tough plants that are used to surviving on very little water.

Such drought-tolerant plants have developed clever adaptations to help them cope with a lack of water; if you recognize these, you'll know which plants to grow.

Many, such as lavender, have gray or silver leaves, which help to reflect the heat of the sun and conserve water. Others, for example lambs' ears (*Stachys byzantina*), produce leaves with tiny hairs that trap moisture. Plants such as pines (*Pinus*) have small, needle-like leaves with a tiny leaf surface so they lose less water, while succulent plants like sedum have leaves that can hold onto water for a long time.

Even though you can improve dry sites by digging in lots of organic matter to increase the soil's moisture-holding capacity, it's still also wise to opt for plants that are known for their tolerance to drought (see box right). These plants are also a good idea if you are growing in shallow planters such as gutters or pocket planters (see pp60–5), or you are not going to be able to devote enough time to watering.

Opposite: **Drought-tolerant plants** have adapted to dry conditions, and many produce succulent leaves, which can hold water for a long time.

TOP DROUGHT-TOLERANT PLANTS

Trees
Acacia dealbata
Cercis siliquastrum

Shrubs
Artemisia "Powis Castle"
Buxus sempervirens
Ceanothus "Blue Mound"
Cistus × *hybridus*
Hebe pinguifolia
Lavandula angustifolia
Nandina domestica
Perovskia "Blue Spire"

Perennials
Echinops ritro "Veitch's Blue"
Erigeron karvinskianus
Eryngium bourgatii
Euphorbia epithymoides
Osteospermum spp.
Sedum Herbstfreude Group
   "Herbstfreude," *S. telephium*
Stachys byzantina
Verbena rigida

Grasses
Briza media
Panicum virgatum
Pennisetum villosum
Stipa tenuissima

Annuals
Bidens ferulifolia
Felicia amelloides
Lantana camara
Nicotiana sylvestris
Plectranthus coleoides
   "Marginatus"

Succulents
Aeonium "Zwartkop"
Echeveria agavoides
Sedum "Dazzleberry"
Sempervivum spp.

Below left: **The fleshy leaves** of *Sedum* "Matrona" conserve water to help the plant thrive during dry weather.

Below right: **Mediterranean plants** such as silver-leaved lavender are a great choice for a dry spot.

CLIMBERS FOR SMALL SPACES

Climbers are the perfect plants for a small space because they have a tiny footprint and yet can green an entire boundary, screen, or arch, often very quickly. They are ideal for hiding an ugly view or for scrambling up and over a wall, and many produce stunning flowers to add a flash of color and even scent. Evergreen climbers (see box right) are the obvious choice for year-round cover.

Climbing plants all cling naturally in different ways. Some such as ivy (*Hedera*) self-cling with suckers or aerial roots and don't need support, but others such as roses (which scramble with thorns) or clematis (which climb by twining tendrils) need trellis or wires to help them clamber up your wall or fence.

If the climbers you choose need support, always put this in place before planting. Make sure any trellis is held 30cm (12in) above the soil to prevent it from rotting, and space horizontal wires 30–40cm (12–16in) apart across your wall or fence. Leave a 30–45cm (12–18in) gap between the plant and the wall or fence so that the

plant's roots can spread and catch any available rainfall.

Immediately after planting, start to train the young stems up bamboo canes held in a fan shape against the wall or fence, so that the plant grows out evenly. Keep tying in new growth until it is growing along the wires or trellis unaided.

TOP CLIMBERS FOR CONFINED AREAS

Evergreen climbers
Clematis armandii, C. cirrhosa var. *purpurascens* "Freckles"
Eccremocarpus scaber
Hedera colchica vars and cvs, *H. helix*
Passiflora caerulea
Solanum crispum "Glasnevin"
Sollya heterophylla
Trachelospermum jasminoides "Variegatum"

Deciduous climbers
Actinidia kolomikta
Akebia quinata
Ampelopsis brevipedunculata
Campsis radicans
Hydrangea anomala subsp. *petiolaris*
Jasminum officinale
Lonicera periclymenum
Muehlenbeckia complexa
Parthenocissus henryana
Rosa: compact climbers cvs, e.g. "Dortmund" (for a shady wall) or "New Dawn" (for a sunny one)
Tropaeolum speciosum

Below left: **Chocolate vine** (*Akebia quinata*) is a twining climber that bursts into spicy, fragrant bloom in spring.

Below center: **Evergreen clematis** are always a good choice and C. x *cartmanii* "Joe" is a compact variety, just the thing for scrambling over a low screen or wall.

Below right: **Although deciduous**, hops (*Humulus*) and Boston ivy (*Parthenocissus tricuspidata*) still make a stunning garden contribution for most of the year.

TREES FOR SMALL SPACES

Every garden should have at least one tree. Standing tall above other plants, it brings structure, shade, color, scent, even fruit, and provides an invaluable habitat for all manner of wildlife. Many trees are beautiful enough to be features in their own right, as specimens in a pot or strategically placed as a screen or focal point, drawing the eye.

Fortunately many will grow happily in pots, and there are plenty of beautiful, small trees that will bring color and vitality to a small area (see box right).

TOP SMALL TREES

- *Acer capillipes*, *A. griseum*
- *Amelanchier canadensis*, *A. lamarckii*
- *Arbutus unedo*
- *Cercis canadensis* "Forest Pansy"
- *Cornus kousa*, *C. mas*
- *Crataegus persimilis* "Prunifolia"
- *Laburnum* spp.
- *Malus transitoria*, *M. trilobata*, *M. × zumi* "Golden Hornet"
- *Prunus serrula*
- *Sorbus* "Eastern Promise"

Top left: **All rowan (*Sorbus*) are beneficial trees** for small spaces with their berries, autumn color, and huge wildlife value.

Top center: **With its deep purple leaves** and pretty pink flowers, Eastern redbud (*Cercis canadensis* "Forest Pansy") is an asset to any garden.

Top right: **Amelanchiers have it all** — dainty spring flowers, vivid autumn leaf tints, and a graceful, upright habit.

Above left: **Acers are a favorite** in many small gardens. They are happy in pots or in the ground, as long as they have a sheltered spot.

Above center: *Malus transitoria* **is a fantastic tree** for the small garden, with its low, spreading habit and mass of fruit.

Above right: **The petal-like bracts of dogwood** (*Cornus kousa*) are followed by crimson leaves in autumn.

Clockwise from top left: **Lady's mantle** (*Alchemilla mollis*), **Geranium** "Johnson's Blue," **heather** (*Calluna vulgaris*), and **periwinkle** (*Vinca difformis*) are all effective groundcover plants.

GROUND COVER

Low-growing plants that form dense carpets of green are brilliant for quickly filling gaps and bringing color to spaces that would otherwise be gray (see box right). They are the perfect choice for tricky spots beneath trees and on sloping ground. Groundcover plants are a great low-maintenance option because they act as a living mulch, keeping down weeds and stopping water evaporating from the soil.

TOP GROUNDCOVER PLANTS

- *Ajuga reptans* "Atropurpurea"
- *Alchemilla mollis*
- *Calluna vulgaris*
- *Campanula poscharskyana*
- *Geranium* "Johnson's Blue"
- *Leucothoe* Scarletta = "Zeblid"
- *Pachysandra terminalis*
- *Pulmonaria rubra*
- *Stachys byzantina* "Silver Carpet"
- *Vinca minor* "Atropurpurea"

SPEEDY PLANTS

When you possess only a few pots, or have a wall to green or a view to hide, you need your plants to grow quickly. If you want to green the space rapidly, then quick growers are the answer (see box opposite). Such speedy plants are also ideal for filling a gap, scrambling across a wall, or providing a bite to eat fast.

Be warned — don't plant too many of them. Some of these vigorous growers may get out of hand in a very small space.

MULTISEASON PERFORMERS

When space is at a premium and you don't have room for many plants, everything you grow has to earn its place. This is an especially important consideration when your green space is an extension of your house, or an outdoor room, because it's nice to have something beautiful nearby that you can look at every day of the year.

Plants with a fleeting flowering period may be lovely for a few days but they are a waste of precious growing space for the rest of the time. Those that provide interest for as much of the year as possible are a better choice. Look for shrubs that have flowers and fruit, trees with interesting bark as well as leaf color, and herbaceous perennials that die back gracefully and with style. There are too many to list here (see box opposite), but if you bear this point in mind when you're shopping for plants, you'll reap the rewards year-round.

TOP SPEEDY PLANTS

Quick herbaceous perennials
Euphorbia griffithii "Fireglow"
Geranium wallichianum and other spp.
Miscanthus sinensis
Perovskia "Blue Spire"
Persicaria amplexicaulis

Climbers
Clematis spp.
Eccremocarpus scaber
Hedera spp.
Humulus lupulus

Annuals
Calendula spp.
Helianthemum spp.
Lathyrus spp.
Nigella spp.
Tropaeolum majus

Vegetables
Beans
Beet
Carrot
Zucchini
Radish
Lettuce

Above: **Sunflowers** (*Helianthus*) are wonderful, speedy annuals that can reach jaw-dropping heights in just a few weeks.

TOP MULTISEASON PLANTS

- *Amelanchier lamarckii*
- *Anemanthele lessoniana*
- *Brunnera macrophylla* "Jack Frost"
- *Cornus alba* "Sibirica," *C. sanguinea* "Midwinter Fire"
- *Erysimum* "Bowles's Mauve"
- *Geranium* "Johnson's Blue"
- *Heuchera* cvs
- × Heucherella cvs
- *Nandina domestica*
- *Skimmia* × *confusa* "Kew Green," *S. japonica* subsp. *reevesiana*
- *Trachelospermum jasminoides*
- *Veronicastrum virginicum*

Left: **Confederate jasmine** (*Trachelospermum jasminoides*) has something to offer year-round. Its glossy, evergreen leaves turn bronze and copper in winter, and it has scented, starry flowers throughout summer.

Above left: **Hoverflies** might look like wasps but they are true flies and brilliant pollinators throughout spring, summer, and autumn.

Above center: **Bees** are often to be found buzzing around the flowers of field scabious (*Knautia arvensis*) in summer.

Above right: **Birds** are a delight to watch, and they are also effective pest controllers because they eat a wide range of insects. .

PLANTS FOR WILDLIFE

One of the most rewarding and invaluable things about turning gray space into green is the impact it has on local wildlife.

Gardens and other green spaces play an essential role in promoting biodiversity. The plants you grow are potential food and shelter for wildlife, so almost any plant is useful. However when you choose them with care you can create an optimum haven for wildlife (see box right). It is not essential to grow solely native plants. In fact it has recently been proven that having a broad mix of both native and non-native plants is the best way to attract wildlife.

Other tips to attract wildlife include the following:

- If you have the space, opt for a range of different types of plants — trees, shrubs, climbers, perennials, annuals, and bulbs.
- Grow nectar-rich plants with single flowers rather than overblown doubles, which have little or no pollen or nectar to offer.
- Look for a range of plants that flower early and late in the season, to provide nectar and pollen for as long a season as possible.
- Select plants that produce berries and seedheads to provide food in autumn. This will help birds and small mammals to survive winter.

Left: **Bees are essential pollinators** in our gardens, transferring pollen from one flower to another and enabling plants to set fruit and seed.

TOP WILDLIFE PLANTS

- *Clematis tangutica* cvs, *C. vitalba* cvs
- *Cotoneaster horizontalis*
- *Crataegus persimilis* "Prunifolia"
- *Crocus* spp.
- *Hedera helix* and cvs
- *Lavandula angustifolia* cvs
- *Lonicera periclymenum* cvs
- *Pyracantha* spp.
- *Sedum spectabile*
- *Sorbus aucuparia*
- *Symphyotrichum* (formerly Aster "Little Carlow"), *S. novi-belgii*
- *Thymus* spp.

EDIBLES FOR SMALL SPACES

Any fruit and vegetables that can be cultivated in a container can be grown in other small spaces (see box below). Fresh salad and herbs will thrive in windowboxes, chilies will ripen in a hanging basket, and an old wheelbarrow can support an entire vegetable plot. Even fruit trees will blossom in a pot, provided you choose the rootstock with care.

Most crops give the best harvest when grown in full sun, but there are plenty that tolerate shade (see box right) and others may crop a little less.

Always provide your fruit and vegetable plants with the biggest containers that you can. Water and feed them regularly to ensure all your hard work rewards you with as big a harvest as possible.

Look for varieties specifically for containers. Also seek out crops that take less time to mature and are quick to harvest and so require less space in the ground. Opt for cherry rather than beefsteak tomatoes, early salad potatoes over maincrop ones, and radishes, carrots, beets, and lettuces that are all speedy growers to give you a delicious crop — fast.

TOP CROPS FOR SHADE

- **Beans**
- **Beets**
- **Blackcurrant**
- **Herbs**: chervil, mint, parsley
- **Peas**
- **Radish**
- **Raspberry**
- **Salads**
- **Spinach**

TOP CROPS FOR SMALL BEDS AND POTS

- **Roots**: carrots, beets, radishes, new potatoes (e.g. "Winston," "Pixie')
- **Lettuce and salad leaves**
- **Herbs**: mint, horseradish, chives, cilantro, parsley, basil
- **Fruit**: strawberries, currants, blueberries, gooseberries, any trees grown on the appropriate dwarf rootstocks
- **Peas and beans**: broad, runner, French, dwarf
- **Green onions**
- **Chilies**: compact and container varieties (e.g. "Pot Black," "Apache," "Fiesta")
- **Tomatoes**: cherry and bush varieties (e.g. "Sungold," "Tumbler")
- **Zucchini**: compact and climbing varieties (e.g. "Black Forest," "Tromboncino')
- **Spinach and chard**

Below: **However small your space**, children can still have fun outside with this edible, scented bucket. When filled with tasty herbs and salads it will pique both their curiosity and their imagination.

Above: **Just a few minutes' care a day**, watering and deadheading, will ensure your plants thrive.

WHAT PLANTS NEED

You may not be able to provide your plants with ideal conditions but you can control their soil, food, and water. When you get these crucial needs right, your plants should be well on their way to being strong and healthy, wherever they're grown.

SOIL & POTTING MIX
Ensure your plants have the very best soil you can give them. Know what type you have in your garden — whether it is sticky clay or gritty, free-draining sand — and dig in plenty of organic

matter or pea gravel to improve it. A soil testing kit will help you establish whether your soil is acidic or alkaline, and once you know this let it dictate the plants you grow.

If you're cultivating in pots, choose good-quality potting mix. Multipurpose soilless ones are perfectly satisfactory for most plants but they do vary in quality, so don't instinctively opt for the cheapest. Soil-based potting mixes are more expensive and heavier than multipurpose ones, but they hold onto

water and nutrients for longer. This is good for perennial plants, which are going to be in a pot for a long time, and for tall plants that might otherwise topple over.

Don't be tempted to use ordinary garden soil in pots. It may contain pests and diseases. Because plants in pots are already under stress, they will succumb quickly.

Always tailor the potting mix to each plant's needs. For example, if you wish to grow acid-loving blueberries or rhododendrons, plant them only in specialist ericaceous compost. If your plant selection calls for free-draining soil, mix in some horticultural pea gravel and organic matter.

WATER

Water is critical to a plant's survival. It aids photosynthesis, provides food in the form of sugars, and helps a plant remain strong and healthy. Without water a plant starts to wilt, the leaves turn pale, the stems become weak, and eventually the plant dies. Most plants, especially those that are grown in containers, will be reliant on you to help them through times of hot weather.

To see whether a plant needs watering, carefully check the soil with a trowel pushed deep into the ground. If it is dry, apply water (see p158). You should not, however, allow plants to become waterlogged. Many of them like free-draining soil, even if they prefer moisture, so add drainage

Below left: **Mulching around plants** with shredded bark will help to conserve water and keep down weeds.

Below right: **Adding slow-release feed** and a little water-retaining gel to soil at planting time ensures plants have a regular supply of nutrients and moisture.

material to the base of pots (see box on p139) and ensure your soil has a good, airy structure.

MULCH

Mulching is crucial in the battle against drought. A layer that sits on the surface of the soil or potting mix, mulch helps to lock in moisture so it can't be lost through evaporation. It also suppresses weeds, creates a barrier against pests, and helps to insulate roots.

Inorganic mulches include stones, pebbles, slate, and crushed shells. Organic mulches such as home-made compost, chipped bark, leafmold, and well-rotted animal manure have the added benefit of feeding your plants as they break down.

Ideally you should water or wait for rain before you mulch the soil.

LIGHT

Plants need sunlight in order to photosynthesize, so don't overcrowd them. A lack of light causes plants to get leggy and lanky as they strain upwards in search of sunlight. Leaves will turn pale (plants with dark or purple leaves will lose their color and revert to green), growth will become distorted, and flowering and

fruiting will fail. Conversely, growing plants that prefer shade in too much light can cause leaves to scorch, so always choose the right plants for any particularly shady spot.

FOOD

Plants require three major nutrients for good health: nitrogen (N) for leafy growth; phosphorus (P) for roots and shoot growth; and potassium (K) for flowers and fruit. Some micronutrients such as magnesium and calcium are also just as vital. Multipurpose potting mix contains enough nutrients for about six weeks, so if plants are to grow in it for longer than this, they will require extra feeding (see p160).

General-purpose fertilizer contains all the major nutrients and many of the lesser ones, and there are potassium-rich feeds such as tomato fertilizer, which promote flowering and fruiting. Seaweed, chicken pellets, and blood, fish and bone are good, all-round organic fertilizers.

A quick-release liquid feed gives plants a short boost, or else you can add a slow-release granular fertilizer when planting and again in spring, as a regular feed throughout the growing season.

HOW TO PLANT

Many of the new plants you introduce into your space will be young and particularly vulnerable to any change in growing conditions. They therefore need to be planted carefully to ensure they get the best possible start, whether planted into containers or directly in the ground. Plant them as soon as you can, and meanwhile keep them well watered.

PLANTING IN THE GROUND

1. Water your plant while it is still in its pot.
2. Dig a hole that is the same depth as the plant's rootball and at least three times its width. Fork through the base and the sides of the hole, to loosen the soil.
3. Remove your plant from its pot and tease out the roots.
4. Place the plant in the hole, making sure that the soil mark on bare-root plants or the top of the potting mix on container plants is level with the soil surface. Fill in around the rootball with soil, firming as you go.
5. Water the plant well.

PLANTING IN A CONTAINER

1. Water your plant while it is still in its original container.
2. Line the base of a new container with drainage material (see p139).
3. Mix horticultural pea gravel, slow-release fertilizer, or water-retaining gel into your potting mix (see p154), depending on the plant's particular needs.
4. Partly fill the lined container with potting mix, leaving enough room for your plant to go in at the same depth as in its previous pot.
5. Remove your plant from its pot and tease apart its roots, then place in the pot, filling in around the rootball with potting mix, and firming down. Make sure there is a 2cm (¾in) gap between the top of the potting mix and the rim of the pot to make watering easier.
6. Water thoroughly, then mulch the surface (see p155).

Above: **Firm down plants when planting**, leaving space at the top of the container to make watering easier.

Below left: **Having removed a plant from its pot,** tease the roots apart before planting it.

Below center: **Once the plant is in the planting hole** make sure it is at the same depth as it was in its pot.

Below right: **Water in well after planting**. Don't let your new plant dry out, especially before it has established.

SOWING SEED

Annual flowers, hardy and tender bedding plants, vegetables, and perennials can all be sown successfully from seed. There are many more varieties of seed available than there are actual plants, so you will have a wider choice if you grow your plants from seed. Seed is also considerably cheaper, and once you have invested in a seed-sowing kit you will make an enormous saving. Fortunately you don't need much!

Some plant seeds require warm conditions for germination so are best started off indoors under cover, while others could just as easily germinate outside, provided the weather is warm enough, but they will get a head start if sown inside and flower or crop a few weeks earlier. Always check your seeds' needs on the packet instructions before you sow.

Any pot with drainage holes is suitable for sowing seeds — old yogurt pots, recycled toilet paper rolls, and pots made from newspaper serve just as well as conventional plant pots. Modular trays are worth investing in. One seed goes in each cell so there is no need to transfer, or prick out, the young seedlings when the first true leaves appear. This saves time and effort, plus some plants such as sweet peas and cilantro actively dislike the root disturbance involved in pricking out.

STARTING SEED INDOORS

A propagator is handy to give your seeds a good start in optimum conditions, but it is not essential, and a position on a warm, bright windowsill above a radiator is almost as good for promoting successful germination.

1. Fill a small pot or modular tray with potting mix and tap it, to settle it down.
2. Dampen the potting mix using the fine rose on your watering can.
3. Depending on the size of the seed and the instructions on its packet, either make shallow holes and push individual seeds into each one or scatter smaller seeds across the surface of the potting mix.
4. If appropriate to the instructions on the seed packet, cover the seeds with a sprinkling of potting mix and then seal the pot with plastic wrap or an inverted, clear plastic bag held in place with a rubber band. Place on a warm, light windowsill.
5. Ensure the potting mix is kept moist until the seeds germinate.
6. Once seedlings appear remove the plastic covering.
7. When the first true leaves develop, prick out the young plants into individual small pots. Always handle the seedlings by their leaves, and never by their stem.
8. A few weeks later, when roots appear through the hole in the bottom of the pot, pot the young plants on into larger pots.
9. Once there is little risk of frosts the young plants can go outside into their final position, provided they have been hardened off for a few days first. Over the course of a week this involves helping plants get used to the change in temperature and conditions outside by placing them outdoors during the day and then bringing them back indoors at night. Finally, plant them out in the morning, to give them the rest of the day to settle in.

SOWING SEEDS IN THE GROUND

Many seeds can be direct sown outside when the conditions are right. This is usually as the days and the soil start to warm up in mid-spring.

Below: **Once seedlings** (here, tomatoes) have developed their first true leaves they can be pricked out into individual pots.

1. Use a hand rake or your hands to break up any lumps in the soil.
2. Make a shallow drill, or groove, in the soil, or create individual holes at the appropriate depth for larger seeds, according to the instructions on the seed packet.
3. Water the drill before sowing, to prevent small seeds being washed away.
4. Sow pinches of small seed thinly along the drill, or drop larger seeds into their individual holes. Draw the soil over them.
5. Keep the soil moist until the seeds germinate.
6. Once seedlings have their first true leaves and are about 3cm (1¼in) tall, thin them out to the final spacings recommended on the packet instructions.

PLANTING BULBS

Bulbs are great in small spaces. They take up very little room, are easy to look after, and come back year after year. They not only look lovely in dedicated groups but also work beautifully when with other plants.

Above left: **Plant bulbs in autumn** and wait for them to reveal their glory in spring.

Above right: **Growing a mix of bulbs** by layering them on top of each other in pots creates an amazing spring display.

Always plant bulbs the right way up — usually with their pointed tip at the top. If you're unsure, just plant them on their side and they should right themselves as they grow. As a general rule most bulbs are planted at three times their depth.

For a dense, flower-filled display, "lasagna planting" is an exciting way of growing two or three different bulbs together, layering them one on top of another. The layers are planted according to size and flowering time, with the earliest-flowering bulbs going in last, at the top.

1. Plant the largest and latest-flowering bulbs, often tulips, towards the base of the pot.
2. Cover these with a layer of potting mix and then plant the next bulb type. Repeat until all the bulbs have been planted.

WATERING

This will be one of your most important and demanding jobs, particularly if you are growing lots of plants in pots. Plants need checking regularly — every day in hot summers. Never assume that recent rainfall will have done the job for you, especially if plants are in a rain shadow cast by a wall or fence.

If you can, invest in an outdoor faucet and a decent-quality hose. Using a spray gun with a fine rose attachment to water will prevent the soil from becoming compacted with repeated watering.

WATER WISE

- Aim water at plant roots, where it is most needed, and always give plants a thorough soaking on each occasion. Check the soil with your fingers — the surface may look wet while the soil below may still be dry. A good watering once a week is best and will encourage deep-rooting plants.
- To prevent evaporation and leaf scorch, water when the sun is at its lowest, either first thing in the morning or in the early evening.
- Don't overwater. Soil should be moist, not soaking. Water-retaining gels will help potting mix hold onto water for longer but don't use too much. If you overdo it, the gel will push plants out of their pots and cause waterlogging.
- Plastic containers hold water better than terracotta ones, and soil-based potting mix retains water for longer than a multipurpose one.
- Group pots together to help create shade and humidity and to conserve water.

- Collect as much rainwater as you can by diverting downpipes and gutters from the house, nearby buildings, even a shed, into water barrels. You can also recycle bath and washing water from the house as long as you use ecofriendly soap and detergents.
- A drip irrigation system (see box right) is a good idea if you have lots of pots and other containers or are short of time to water regularly and properly. Seep irrigation and porous hoses are also useful.

Top: **Aim to water in the mornings** or evenings, when the sun is low, so that the water won't quickly evaporate.

Above: **Drip irrigation systems** are great for getting water directly to thirsty plants.

IRRIGATION SYSTEMS

If you're pushed for time, have a number of pots, or are simply away from home a lot, then an irrigation system is a wise investment. They deliver water exactly where it's needed — at the base of the plant — and there is no run-off or waste because the water gradually soaks into the soil. A number of different types are available but they will all prove much more convenient if you have an outside faucet.

A hose timer is invaluable if you want to cut down on the chore of watering or wish to ensure your plants are watered when you are not around. It fits between the faucet and the hose and allows you to water at a predetermined time, for a particular duration, such as 2 or 10 minutes. Simple timers can be set to turn the water off after a preset time, while more sophisticated ones have a number of preset programs. These can come on and off more than once during the day and be set to do so over the course of a week or two, helping you to plan watering when you are on vacation.

All timers can be used with the following irrigation systems.

Seep or trickle irrigation

This irrigation system is made up of plastic or rubber hoses that have small holes down one side of their entire length. They are laid on or just under the soil, so water is directed to the base of plants. Seep irrigation systems are particularly good for watering vegetable beds, where plants are grown in rows, or for snaking through ornamental beds and borders.

Above: **A timer** attached to your faucet allows plants to be watered when you're not around.

Porous hoses

These are similar to trickle systems but the rubber hose is porous all over and seeps water slowly into the soil. It can be buried below the soil surface or under a layer of mulch. As plants are watered directly at their roots there is no water loss from evaporation, and weed establishment is hindered because the soil surface remains dry. Porous hoses are suitable for use in all beds, including those that slope.

Drip-feed systems

Water flows along the hose and is then fed to plants individually through tubes that are supported by spikes stuck in the ground. Water is dripped or sprayed gently onto the soil surface next to the plant. This focused watering is perfect for use in pots and small beds, and for placing right under specific plants that need regular watering.

FEEDING

Plants make their own food by photosynthesizing — using the sun's energy to create simple sugars from carbon dioxide and water. Using those sugars as a fuel, the plant goes on to manufacture more complex molecules using nutrients extracted from the soil by the roots. These nutrients can run out, particularly if the plants are growing in pots (see p154). Then feeding becomes as essential as watering (see p158).

To ensure your soil is nutrient rich, dig in plenty of well-rotted organic matter. Both horse and cattle manure contain lots of nutrients and can be added before planting or used under mulch at the base of established plants. Always leave a 10cm (4in) gap around each stem base.

Granular fertilizers are handy. They can be pushed into the soil in pots or around the base of plants, or just sprinkled on top, or else you can mix slow-release granular feeds into potting mix at planting time (see p156). They will provide plants with nutrients until the end of the season.

Quick-release liquid fertilizers supply nutrients in a quick boost and are easy to apply — just add them to a watering can before you water your plants. They provide nutrients in a form that can be readily absorbed. The most common liquid feeds are high-potassium ones, which promote fruiting and flowering.

Although there are lots of chemical fertilizers, you can make your own for a free and steady supply of organic, nutrient-rich feed.

MAKE YOUR OWN FERTILIZER

Comfrey (*Symphytum × uplandicum*) plants have long root systems, which access nutrients deep in the soil and store them in their leaves. They are rich in potassium (K) and also contain potash (P) and nitrogen (N). In fact they have a higher NPK content than farmyard manure. Conveniently you can turn comfrey leaves into an amazing potassium-rich plant food. The best variety to plant is the Russian "Bocking 14," which is sterile and so can't set seed and take over your garden.

Once plants have established, harvest some of the leaves, chop them roughly, and soak them in a bucket of water covered with a lid for a few weeks. They will break down into a rich, dark (smelly) liquid that can be diluted one part comfrey liquid to ten parts water and then fed to your plants.

Below left: **Slow-release feeds** sprinkled into potting mix will provide nutrients for the entire growing season.

Below right: **Liquid fertilizers** give plants a boost when they need it and are great for increasing crop yield and flowers.

Left: If you have the room, it's worth having a compost bin. There are some lovely ones available that won't dominate a small space.

WHAT TO PUT IN YOUR COMPOST HEAP

For optimum decomposition, add a mix of "green," nitrogen-rich waste and "brown," carbon-rich material. Aim for 25–50 percent green waste and the rest can be brown.

Green waste

Flowers
Fruit
Grass clippings
Leaves
Prunings
Tea bags
Vegetable peelings

Brown waste

Cardboard
Eggshells
Hair
Shredded paper
Straw
Wood ash

Turning your compost

Turning your compost once a month can be the difference between compost being ready in 6 months as opposed to a year. Ideally, dump out a bin or fork out a heap completely and mix it all up before replacing it. That said, just forking through the layers so that the material on the outside is turned into the middle will still make a difference.

COMPOSTING

If you have even the tiniest bit of spare space, devote it to a compost heap to recycle your kitchen and paper waste and make a good soil-improver for your garden — for free. When added to the soil, particularly along with well-rotted manure or spent mushroom compost, garden compost boosts nutrient levels, increases the soil's ability to hold onto those nutrients, and improves drainage and aeration.

Make your own compost heap with boards or buy a store-made version. The bigger the composting bin or heap, the better the compost will be.

If you find your small space is simply not generating enough green waste, a wormery, which composts mainly kitchen waste, is a great alternative.

Place your bin or heap in a shady spot, preferably directly on the ground. If that's not possible, add a layer of soil to the bottom of your bin.

Try to add green and brown waste (see right) in layers, and don't have too much of either one. Air is essential in a heap, to get the composting process going, so turn your compost regularly (see right). When your compost is ready, it should be dark and crumbly with a sweet, earthy smell.

PRUNING TIPS

Pruning is a necessary gardening task. It keeps plants in check, improves their shape, encourages new growth and better flowering and fruiting, and maximizes their health. Always use clean, sharp tools. When you prune depends on the individual plant and why you are cutting it.

TREES

Deciduous trees are generally pruned in the dormant season, between late autumn and early spring. Aim for a balanced, attractively shaped tree, by first snipping out diseased, damaged, and dead wood and then any crossing and rubbing growth. Cut to an outward-facing bud and take care not to cut stems too close to the trunk, because healing may be difficult.

Evergreen trees need little pruning: just remove dead and diseased wood in late summer.

HERBACEOUS PERENNIALS

Most herbaceous plants can be cut down to just above ground level once they have finished flowering and their stems start to fade. Leave any that have attractive seedheads because these will provide food and homes for wildlife through the winter. They can then be cut down as new growth starts again in spring.

SHRUBS & CLIMBERS

Most evergreen shrubs and climbers require little pruning, while deciduous ones are pruned according to when they flower. As a general rule of thumb, those that bloom before the end of June (e.g. weigela and philadelphus) are cut back right after flowering, and those that flower from July onwards (e.g. *Spiraea japonica* and perovskia) are cut back in spring.

CLEMATIS

All clematis are pruned depending on when they flower and they are grouped accordingly.

MAKING THE RIGHT CUT

When pruning, it is crucial that you cut with care. If you get it wrong, buds won't grow or whole stems may die back.

Make an angled cut just above a bud that is pointing in the direction you want it to grow. Always snip just above a bud — not too close or you will damage it.

The angled cut should face the same way as the bud. This allows water to run away from the bud and also triggers growth hormones to be directed into the bud.

Below left: **Herbaceous perennials** that don't develop attractive seedheads or have hollow stems can be cut down to the base in autumn.

Below center: **Always cut just above** an outward-facing bud, to encourage the plant to branch out and have an open center.

Below right: **Cut back spring-flowering** shrubs, such as this weigela, right after flowering.

Group 1 (e.g. *Clematis* alpina, *C. armandii*, *C. cirrhosa*, *C. montana*): These flower in winter and early spring on shoots that are produced the previous summer. Plants don't need pruning every year but they can be cut back after flowering to keep them in check.

Group 2 (e.g. *Clematis* "Barbara Jackman," *C. florida* var. *florida* "Sieboldiana," *C.* "Multi Blue," *C.* "Nelly Moser'): These large-flowered hybrid varieties flower from early summer on last year's growth. Cut stems back in spring just before they start into growth, but do not cut too much or they will lose their potential flowers.

Group 3 (e.g. *Clematis tangutica*, *C. texensis*, *C. viticella*): These late summer- and autumn-flowering clematis bloom on the current season's growth. They are the easiest to prune: cut all the stems back to one or two buds, about 15cm (6in) above ground level, in late winter or early spring.

BULBS

Bulbs need their leaves in order to photosynthesize and generate food for the following year, so do not be tempted to cut or even tie back the leaves once the flowers have faded. Wait until the leaves themselves have turned yellow and straw-like, about six weeks after flowering, before cutting them back.

Right: **Group 3 clematis** such as this stunning *C.* "Margot Koster" are the easiest to prune. Simply snip their stems just above ground level in spring.

PLANT PROTECTION

Even though your plants may be growing strongly and healthily, it is important to continue to nurture them in as helpful an environment as possible. By protecting them, particularly when they are young or first planted, you will help them settle in quickly, but plant protection offers other benefits too.

- Increasing the temperatures around plants with horticultural fleece or cloches will speed up growth and promote earlier flowering or a longer cropping period compared with unprotected plants.
- Protection at the end of the growing season and before the first frosts will insulate more tender plants against winter cold.

Below left: **Traditional bell cloches** are an attractive way to protect young plants against inclement weather in spring and at the end of the season.

Below right: **A fleece tunnel** will protect brassicas against the cold and will also prevent birds from pecking the leaves.

- Erecting protective barriers will keep pests and diseases off your plants. Lift covers on warm days to give plants a good airing.
- Protecting and warming the soil before planting or seed sowing will allow you to plant or sow a little earlier in the season and will reduce the shock for plants.

Cloches: These protective structures are traditionally made of transparent plastic or glass, often in the shape of a bell or tunnel (or they can be home-made from a plastic bottle or jar). Cloches work like tiny greenhouses, protecting plants against the weather and raising the temperature within. They can be used to extend the flowering and cropping seasons as well as reduce airborne diseases. Ensure plants are well ventilated and watered by lifting cloches on warm, bright days. Plastic cloches need to be fixed to the ground.

Containers: Group these together in the shade to shield them from summer heat. Placing them together raises humidity levels and reduces moisture loss. In winter, move pots

to warmer positions and insulate them with bubble wrap, to protect plant roots against the cold.

Horticultural fleece: This soft, white, transparent material helps protect plants against the cold. It is useful for tender plants planted in spring and for helping other plants survive winter when it is wrapped around them in autumn, often with straw.

Mulching: A thick layer of organic matter (see p155) around the base of plants helps retain water in summer and stops plant roots from freezing in winter, particularly plants in pots. It can also deter some pests.

Netting: Bird- and insect-proof mesh netting is useful in preventing crops, leaves, and flower buds from being eaten. It should be stretched tautly around a plant so that birds do not become ensnared. Netting offers some weather protection but does not raise temperatures.

COMPANION PLANTING
It is believed that certain plants grown together can help each other in some way. These companion plants are thought to encourage beneficial insects, deter or repel pests, or sacrifice themselves by attracting pests from another plant.

Borage and lavender are popular with pollinating bees and butterflies, while lavender's strong scent is also said to confuse pests. Cilantro too has a strong scent, which may deter aphids; dill and fennel are reputed to attract aphid-eating hoverflies, while garlic chives may mask the smell of carrots from carrot fly and repel aphids from raspberries.

COMMON PROBLEMS & SOLUTIONS

The happier the plant, the healthier it will be and so less vulnerable to attack from pests and diseases. Good growing techniques help you produce the strongest, healthiest plants.

- Don't overdo the watering and feeding of your plants. Too much water causes waterlogging (see p158) and too much fertilizer, especially nitrogen, produces weak, lax stems that are prone to attack by pests (see p160).
- Grow plants in the optimum-quality soil or potting mix.
- Always grow plants in a place appropriate to their cultural needs. When you choose a plant to suit your particular situation it will be all the happier for it — and easier to look after.

Right: **Creating a barrier** between young plants and slugs and snails may deter these pests attacking your plants. Coffee grounds sprinkled around plants are unpleasant for them to travel across, so they should leave your plants alone. Just be sure to replace the grounds after rain.

- Don't overcrowd plants. Poor air circulation raises humidity and causes fungal diseases (see p166) and weak growth.
- Research what can cause your plants harm and use barriers to protect them (see p164).

Inevitably the odd problem or pest attack will occur. Fortunately the main offenders are fairly predictable so be vigilant and try to spot them early, to keep damage to a minimum.

PESTS

Aphids, including greenfly and blackfly, love soft, new growth so are mainly a problem in spring. Although they won't kill plants they do weaken them and also spread viruses and some diseases. Let nature take them

in hand by encouraging their natural predators — ladybugs, lacewings, and hoverflies — into the garden. If only a few plants are affected, rub aphids off by hand. Hosing them off with insecticidal soap will also work.

Beetles that cause problems include the sparkling rosemary beetle, which loves both rosemary and lavender, and the bright scarlet lily beetle. Look for them from spring to autumn, and for their larvae on the undersides of leaves from autumn to spring. If you spot them, tap them onto newspaper held beneath plants or pick them off by hand one at a time.

Birds, primarily pigeons, can be a serious problem to plants, ripping and tearing leaves and reducing them

Far left: **Snails are a common menace** in most gardens, particularly in spring, when they love munching on young, juicy foliage.

Left: **Adult vine weevils** leave distinctive notches on leaf edges but usually only come out at night.

to bare, stunted stems. Use cloches to protect young plants, or stretch horticultural fleece or netting over them. Protect edible fruit bushes and trees with netting as soon as they flower. Scaring birds by hanging up CDs or sparkly foil can also work.

Cats are a big problem in urban gardens, where they dig up beds and borders, knock over pots, trample plants, and use any bare ground as a litterbox. To make your garden less attractive to cats, plant closely together and don't leave any bare ground — plant it or cover it with sticks until you do. Water regularly, because cats don't like wet soil, or try some of the commercial cat deterrents.

Slugs & snails are the most common and frustrating problem faced by gardeners — and a particular problem if you garden in a damp, shady spot. Telltale signs include holes in leaves and the all-too-familiar slime trails. There is a plethora of suggested ways to deal with slugs and snails, and the best defense is to try anything and everything.

If you catch these pests, get rid of them by dehydrating them in salt or chopping them with pruning shears and throwing them away.

- Look for slugs and snails at the base of plants and on leaves. Night-time collections with a flashlight are often a very productive way to spot them.
- Trap these pests in beer traps or leave out upturned citrus skins.
- When the weather is consistently warm enough (over 5°C/41°F), water predatory nematodes into the soil.
- Copper tape around pots and raised beds will give slugs and snails an electric shock. Alternatively, smear pot rims with petroleum jelly, which will trap them and stop them from reaching your plants.
- Sprinkle slug pellets around the base of vulnerable plants. Use those containing ferric sulphate (rather than metaldehyde), which is not as toxic and less harmful to children, animals, and wildlife.

Vine weevil: Adult vine weevils and larvae cause damage. The adults are nocturnal, black, and beetle-like.

They feed on foliage and leave characteristic, semicircular notches along the leaf edges. The cream-colored larvae feed on the roots of plants, causing them to wilt and eventually die. They are a particular problem on plants in pots, so look for signs of vine weevil when you buy or repot plants, by lifting plants out of their pots so you can check their roots. Netting or fleece will prevent attack by adult vine weevils or go after them at night with a flashlight and pick them off plants. Encourage predatory birds by putting out feeders and nesting boxes.

PROBLEMS
Blackspot: Fungal diseases such as blackspot are common on roses, where they infect leaves and stems and can reduce plant growth. Look out for black or purple spots and blotches on the upper surface of leaves, which may turn yellow and fall off. Collect and destroy fallen leaves.

Downy mildew: This causes blotches and a gray fuzz on leaves, flowers, and fruit. It thrives in wet weather so don't overwater plants and always water plants at their base and not over the leaves (see p158). Water in the mornings rather than the evenings when conditions are more humid, and don't overcrowd plants so there is good air movement around them.

Nip off any infected areas as soon as you spot them, and dig up severely infected plants.

Powdery mildew: This white mold appears on the upper and lower surface of leaves in dry weather. It is worse when air circulation is poor so don't crowd plants by growing them too close together. Water regularly (see p158) and mulch plants to help retain water in the soil (see p155).

Rust: Orange, brown, or yellow fungal spots on the undersides of leaves occur on lots of different plants, from pelargoniums and roses to leeks. If you spot them, remove infected stems and leaves, and discard them; never put them on the compost heap.

Don't plant too close together, and try not to get plant leaves wet when watering.

WEEDS

Most gardens and containers will be besieged by weeds. They don't just ruin the look of your displays, they also compete with them for food and water. If weeds get really out of hand, they dominate the space and light.

The key to controlling all weeds — both annuals and the more tenacious perennial weeds — is to get on top of them quickly, when they are small and have not had a chance to seed.

Annual weeds such as chickweed, hairy bittercress may live for only a year but they often have fast life cycles and can quickly scatter a lot of seeds, spreading it over your plot year after year. Fortunately annual weeds are easy to kill — cut them off at ground level with a hoe or by hand weeding. For weeds in paths, douse them in boiling water — or Coke on a hot, sunny day. It works surprisingly well.

Perennial weeds such as dandelions, buttercups, bindweed, ground elder, and stinging nettles are deep-rooted plants that die back in winter but return every spring. They are tough to control, because you must remove every last bit of root to get rid of them. If you leave even the tiniest bit of root behind, it will resprout. Hoeing and digging them out will weaken perennial weeds over time; otherwise the use of a systemic weedkiller will knock them back. When resorting to

weedkiller, take particular care around children, animals, and wildlife.

For a more organic approach, cutting back perennial weeds and then smothering them with heavy, black plastic, weed-suppressing membrane, or layers of cardboard and compost blocks out the light and will eventually destroy them. However this takes considerable time, and areas are unusable while you wait.

If weeds are running through your plants, keep picking out the new growth to weaken it or dig up plants in autumn, wash their roots, and clear the area well. Never throw perennial weeds into your compost because they will reinfest your patch.

Below left: **Dandelions in paths** can be particularly tricky to remove because you need to get rid of all the taproot to prevent them from resprouting.

Below center: **Keep hoeing** away weed seedlings such as this nettle and you will weaken the plant and eventually prevent it from growing.

Below right: **Covering the soil** with a layer of mulch such as leaf mold or spent potting mix will help suppress weeds and stop them from taking over beds and borders.

GLOSSARY

Annual A plant that completes its life cycle — germinating, flowering, and dying — in one year.

Anchors Plastic plugs that are put inside a hole in a masonry wall and will expand when a screw is drilled into it.

Aquatic plant basket A pot used for growing aquatic plants in ponds, which has mesh sides to allow water and air to flow through.

Aquatic compost A loam-based compost with a low-nutrient content for aquatic plants.

Bare-root A plant with very little or no soil on its roots when purchased.

Bedding plants Annuals or biennials grown almost to maturity and then planted outside for temporary display through the summer months.

Biennial A plant that completes its life cycle in two years.

Cable tie Flexible plastic strips that "tie" using the ratchet system and hold things together such as bamboo canes.

Cultivar A contraction of "cultivated variety," or cv. Refers to a plant that originated in cultivation rather than in the wild. Is often used interchangeably with the term "variety," or var.

Deadheading The removal of dead or fading flowers to prevent them from going to seed in order to promote further flowering, and to tidy up the plant.

Ericaceous Term describing plants that require acidic soil to grow in, e.g., ferns, blueberries. Also refers to the type of acidic soil (of pH 6.5 or less) that these plants need to grow in.

Eye screw A screw with a loop on one end, through which you insert garden wire or string.

Evapotranspiration The combination of the evaporation of water from the land and the transpiration of water from plants into the atmosphere.

Gabion A wire cage that is filled with rock or concrete in road building and retaining walls but can also be used as a decorative garden feature.

Garden compost Homemade organic material that combines plant material, paper, cardboard, and kitchen scraps left to decay into dark, humus-rich compost used for mulching and improving the soil.

Can also be purchased ready-made at garden centers.

Genus A category in plant classification that describes a group of closely related plants that rank below family and above species.

Ground anchor bolts Metal bolts that secure a structure like a post to the ground by expanding the anchor when the bolt is drilled in.

Grow-bag A commercial plastic bag filled with nutrient-rich potting mix that is used for growing plants, usually hanging against a wall, rather than planting them in a pot or the open ground.

Habitat An area inhabited by a particular species of plant that is its natural environment and is made up of a particular soil, moisture, temperature, and amount of sunlight most beneficial for the plant.

Heat Island effect The effect that human activity within urban areas (e.g., automobiles, concrete buildings) has on the temperature of the area, making it significantly warmer than the surrounding rural areas.

Hurdles (hazel or willow) A woven movable fence panel.

Jigsaw A hand or motorized saw with a thin blade, which enables you to cut intricate details.

Landscape fabric A fabric to suppress weeds, which is permeable to water and moisture.

Loam-based potting mix A soil-based potting mix made from a mixture of loam, peat, and sand with added fertilizers and nutrients. It is heavy and good for stability in pots and is also suitable for thirsty plants, as it holds moisture well.

Lost head (countersunk) screws Screws with small heads on them that can't be seen once screwed into wood.

Manure Well-rotted organic material added to soil or compost to increase fertility or amend soil pH. Usually of animal origin. Available bagged at garden centers.

Mattock A versatile hand tool that combines an axe head and a pick (adze) head which can be used for digging and chopping.

Microclimate An area within a garden where the light, heat or wind conditions differ from the surrounding area, e.g., at the base of a south-facing wall or in a corner.

Mortar Workable paste used to bind brick and stones together. Mainly made out of sand and cement but can also include lime. Available premixed.

Mulch A layer of organic or inorganic material that sits on the soil surface and reduces moisture loss, acts as a barrier against weeds and pests, prevents compaction, and insulates roots against cold weather.

Multipurpose potting mix A mixture of peat, loam, sand, and bark plus some lime and fertilizers. Suitable for sowing and growing a wide range of plants. Available premixed at garden centers.

Native Plants that grow spontaneously within a geographic area and have not been introduced by humans.

Organic matter Composts or similar materials derived from plant materials.

Perennial Any plant that lives for more than two years.

Perlite Small granules of expanded volcanic materials that are added to any soil mixture to improve aeration.

Pollinator An agent (usually an animal, insect, wind) that transfers pollen between parts of a plant which then makes fruit or seeds.

Potting mix A medium for growing plants. There are many different types, including multipurpose, loam-based, and ericaceous. They are made of different constituents depending on the types of plants being grown.

Plug seedlings Plants sold as seedlings or young plants. Available early in the gardening season. An alternative to growing plants from seed.

Pressure-treated lumber Lumber that has been treated with preservative that has been forced deep into the wood using hydraulic pressure.

Rain shadow An area next to a wall or fence that is sheltered from wind, heavy rain and, in some cases, sunshine.

Repotting Term describing the moving of seedlings or young plants into larger pots or the garden to give them room to keep growing.

Root-bound Term describing a plant whose roots have filled a pot, leaving no room for further growth.

Seedhead The capsules or pods that contain a plant's seeds. Many plants, such as ornamental grasses and Eryngium (sea holly), have decorative seedheads and these are left on the plant to provide interest throughout the autumn and winter.

Self-drilling screw A screw with a sharp point or drill head that creates its own hole for easy insertion. Useful in hard materials like wood, plastic and metal.

Shelter belt A line of trees or shrubs planted to protect an exposed area from high winds. Sometimes called a wind break.

Shrub A plant with several woody stems emerging from or near the base but no central trunk.

Slow-release fertilizer Fertilizers that release nutrients slowly into the soil and usually dependent on soil micro-organisms and temperature.

Soilless potting mix A potting mix, usually based on peat rather than soil. Contains different types and amounts of nutrients and fertilizers depending on what it is to be used for: e.g., seeds need fewer nutrients than longer-term plants. Good for small pots, windowboxes, and baskets because of its light weight, but generally requires more watering.

Soil-based potting mix Refers to the range of potting materials that are based predominantly on soil rather than peat. May be sold as all-purpose potting mix.

Species A category in plant classification, below genus, used to describe a specific type of plant.

Succulent A plant with thick fleshy leaves and/or stems that have adapted to store water.

Lumber batten A long, flat strip of rectangular wood used to hold something in place or against a wall.

Topdressing A layer of fresh soil, compost or a mix of both added to the surface of a container or the garden to replenish nutrients. It can be done after removing the top 10–15cm (4–6in) of depleted soil or lightly mixed in. Also refers to the decorative mulch applied to the soil surface around a plant.

Variety A category in plant classification used to describe a group of closely related plants ranked below that of species. Often used more familiarly and interchangeably with *cultivar*.

Waterlogged Almost completely saturated with water near to or at the point of dripping or pooling. No air spaces remain in the soil and any plants growing in it can drown.

Water-retaining gel Granules or crytals added to potting mix that swell to many times their size when wet to increase the ability of the potting mix to retain water.

RESOURCES

Websites for further general information

The Royal Horticultural Society www.rhs.org.uk

The American Horticultural Society www.ahs.org

Books

Planting the Dry Shade Garden: the Best Plants for the Toughest Spot in Your Garden, Graham Rice (Timber Press, 2011)

RHS Grow Your Own Crops in Pots, Kay Maquire (Mitchell Beazley, 2013)

RHS How to Plant a Garden, Matt James (Mitchell Beazley, 2016)

RHS Small Garden Handbook (Making the Most of Your Outdoor Space), Andrew Wilson (Mitchell Beazley, 2013)

RHS The Urban Gardener, Matt James (Mitchell Beazley, 2014)

RHS What Plant When (DK, 2011)

The Dry Garden, Beth Chatto (W&N, 1998)

The RHS A–Z Encyclopedia of Garden Plants, Christopher Brickell (DK, 1996)

The RHS Encyclopedia of Garden Design (DK, 2013)

The RHS Encyclopedia of Plants and Flowers, Christopher Brickell (DK, 2010)

The RHS Plant Finder, Janet Cubey (Royal Horticultural Society, 2015)

The RHS What Plant Where Encyclopedia (DK, 2013)

Shows

Northwest Flower and Garden Show

Canada Blooms

Helpful and inspirational websites:

www.gardenista.com

www.growingwithplants.com

http://garden.org

www.urbanorganicgardener.com

www.frustratedgardener.com

You should find the following are available at all good hardware and DIY stores:

Gutters and brackets

Lumber, screws, and nails

Natural sisal rope

Galvanized chain

Anchor bolts kit

Large S-shaped hooks can be sourced from good kitchen stores.

Crates and fruit boxes are often available from online auction sites and second-hand stores.

Source lumber deckboards from DIY stores and garden centers. Look for the Forest Stewardship Council (FSC), or similar, certification.

INDEX

ACKNOWLEDGMENTS

The publishers would like to thank the following people and suppliers who have helped to make this book possible by generously supplying their time and products:

For providing fantastic locations we would like to thank:

Alex Brown & Oliver Butler

Andrew Merrett

Emma Whale & Matt Powell

Isobel Meadows

Kay & Roger Bromley

Stephen Ladlow

Valerie Russell

William & Zita Gibson

We used a number of kits and planters to help us create some of the projects. This is where we sourced them from:

Pages 64, and 87
Veriplant pocket planters by Burgon & Ball
www.burgonandball.com

Page 66
Living Wall kit "easiwall-pro"
www.treebox.co.uk

Page 72
Western red cedar
www.silvatimber.co.uk

Page 92
Malmesbury planters
www.gardentrading.co.uk

Page 97
Skinny balcony planters
www.gardenclublondon.co.uk

Page 111
Water bowl pot
www.worldofpots.com

Pages 19 and 114
Retro steel raised bed kit
www.harrodhorticultural.com

Page 116
Living roof sedum mat
www.enviromat.co.uk

Page 125
Gabion kit
www.landscapeplus.com

Tony would like to thank:

My family and close team who supported me and helped to make the projects happen including Lizzy Woods, Fillipo Dester, and Andrea Fantini.

Kay would like to thank:

I couldn't have written this book without the love and support from Jo, Kipling, and Matilda. Thank you.

Picture credits:

All photographs © Jason Ingram with the exception of pages 7, 28, 40, 42, 45a, ar, bl, c, cl & cr, 47ac, bl & br, 48, 49, 88ar & b, 121ar & bl, 166 which are © Jason Ingram/BBC Gardeners' World